MW01293104

Couples in Crisis: Overcoming Affairs & Opposite-Sex Friendships

A Fast & Innovative Approach to Rebuild Trust

& Revive Your Marriage (Not Talk It To Death)

Debra Macleod, B.A., LL.B.

Cover Illustration:

Lost love & love sickness. © Thomas Bethge. Provided by Shutterstock.com

Inside illustrations:

Mobile phone. © ladynoi. Provided by Shutterstock.com

Couple speaking at the phone. © IsaArt. Provided by Shutterstock.com

Castle. © NEGOVURA. Provided by Shutterstock.com

Family inside the house. © IsaArt. Provided by Shutterstock.com

TABLE OF CONTENTS

Introduction: To Be Read By Both Spouses

"Calm down, Chrissy! I'm not cheating on you. Do you see anything in this text about having sex? We're just talking about work and making a few jokes. Christ, why are you so paranoid and controlling? She's just a friend. Deal with it."

"You should be talking to me, I'm your wife! I don't trust her. Why do I feel like she's more important to you than I am?"

• • •

Jessica collapsed in tears on the bed. It had been over a month since her husband Tom had admitted he had slept once with a woman he worked with. He said it was over, but the slut kept calling and texting and he kept leaving the room to reply to her in private.

It was always some "crisis" in her life – her car broke down, her furnace wasn't working, she was having a meltdown, whatever. And every time it happened, Tom would say, "What do you expect me to do? She's not a bad person, I can't just leave her stranded. She's a single mom and she needs me." He actually defended her!

It had gotten so bad that Tom had moved into the basement. Jessica missed him but whenever she asked whether he was willing to end it once and for all, he'd say, "I don't know…I'm not sure how I feel…I need more time."

• • •

Matt stared at the pile of wedding RSVP's on the kitchen table. He and Chloe were getting married in one week, but he had just learned from a friend that Chloe had gotten drunk and "made out" with an ex-boyfriend on the night of her bachelorette party.

Chloe swore up and down that it meant nothing. It was just a stupid mistake and some meaningless feelings of nostalgia. She said the alcohol had compromised her judgment, and was she begging him to forgive her. She swore up and down that she had done nothing wrong and that it hadn't gone beyond a kiss.

Yet his friend James had said that she and her ex-boyfriend had disappeared from the party for over an hour....

• • •

Paul held his wife's cell phone in his hand and stared, his hands shaking and his stomach contents threatening to come up, at the picture she had sent a man named Jason.

He recognized the name – it was a guy she had met at the gym and had mentioned in passing a few times. She had sent him a picture of herself in the shower, naked, smiling and touching herself. The caption read, "I'm still sore from the other night. Thinking of you xoxo"

• • •

Mike opened the front door and was met by his irate wife, shoving crumpled papers into his chest. "I printed these out from your email account...how long have you been screwing her?"

Mike's stomach dropped. "You went into my email account? That's private!" He knew it was the wrong thing to say, but he was in shock and reacted on impulse. His head was spinning.

His wife picked up the bag at her feet and threw it at him. "Get out."

"This is my house, too. Those are my kids."

"Get out, or I'll call a lawyer and this will get a lot worse."

In a swirl of emotion – anger, fear, shock – Mike picked up the bag and left, his wife slamming the door behind him. He thought he caught a glimpse of his five-year-old son as the door closed.

When it comes to emotional or sexual affairs, inappropriate opposite-sex friendships and other indiscretions, there are a thousand scenarios and dialogues like these, each more gut-wrenching and heart-breaking than the last.

No doubt you have your own scenario and dialogue. No doubt they have left you feeling shocked, sickened and questioning everything you thought you knew about your partner and your life.

Well, you're not alone. I wrote this book because the vast majority of my clients now present with a trust-related crisis. Other marriage problems – communication, money, in-laws, etc. – pale in comparison to the turmoil and frequency of infidelity, particularly today's "new infidelity" which is facilitated by personal technology (i.e. phone texting, computers), online activities and social media.

But fear not. By working together through this book and this crisis as allies and not enemies, your scenario can be a much happier one – and sooner than you think.

Regardless of what has happened, I applaud you for choosing to target and tackle your problems together. That's what marriage is all about, even when – perhaps *especially* when – those problems seem insurmountable. They aren't.

"Can We Really Get Past This?"

Of course you can. A crisis of broken trust – whether a full-blown affair or an online indiscretion – need not define your entire marriage or relationship or set a permanent tone.

Your relationship is bigger than what you're going through right now.

You both had the best of intentions when you started out and for whatever reasons things have fallen off the rails. But it's never too late to get back on-track and start moving forward again.

Indeed, some couples who have recovered from infidelity say that their marriage is stronger for it. They see it as a wake-up call that alerted them to their marriage problems.

Without that wake-up call, they would have kept sleeping at the wheel, kept driving their relationship into the ditch, until an even bigger crash – divorce – was unavoidable.

Whether you recover from this crisis of broken trust is entirely up to you. Rather, it's up to the both of you. Recovery takes love, maturity, empathy, humility, patience, perspective and a willingness to change.

It takes the two of you, acting as allies.

"We Want To Get Past It, But We Are Hurt, Afraid, Overwhelmed And Confused...What Do We Do?"

You take a deep breath, pour yourself a cup of coffee, curl up on the couch and start reading.

Despite the emotional chaos you may be feeling – shock, fear, anger, betrayal, regret, guilt, sadness, confusion and so on – there is still love between you.

It may not be as palpable as other feelings right now, but it's still there. If it weren't, you wouldn't be reading this book.

My job is to help you manage this crisis period. My job is to help you navigate your way through everything that has happened, and through everything you both are feeling, so that you can once again make love the prevalent emotion in your relationship.

Love is a foundational emotion. Upon it, we will rebuild trust, devotion, adoration, appreciation, gratitude, intimacy and friendship.

I've been doing my job for a long time. I've had couples present in my office only hours after an infidelity was discovered. I've had couples present after months of useless counselling or talk therapy that only made them feel angrier and more resentful of each other, and more hopeless about their marriage.

I've had people – men and women – burst into tears, collapse in grief, sit in stunned silence and scream into the pillow I keep in my office for those who need to physically vent their rage, regret or heartache before they can focus.

I've had spouses whose hands shook so badly with fear, sadness or shock that they could barely hold a pen to sign a form.

And if they can get past it, so you can you. If they can rediscover their love and rebuild their relationship upon it – often stronger and happier than ever – so can you.

Why "Getting Past It" Is Better Than Giving Up

The truth is, couples who "give up" and break up after a crisis of broken trust often experience a fallout that is more toxic than either one of them expected. Relationship and/or family breakdown often have consequences that people don't anticipate, especially when they are making purely emotion-based decisions.

In addition to the obvious financial setbacks and lifestyle changes, people with children may be faced with child custody battles and the loss of control over who is in their children's lives, particularly as their ex-partner begins to date again. They may assume that their relationship with their own children will not change – although it inevitably will, and rarely for the better.

Other people assume that their next relationship or partner will be perfect, or at least much better. Yet as often as not, subsequent partners have their own history of failed relationships, baggage and character shortcomings.

When we're driven by pain, we may think that the grass will be greener on the other side of the fence. We may think that jumping over the fence will take our pain away; however, it's only once we've committed to jumping over the fence that we sometimes realize the other grass has even more painful thistles.

Many people who "give up" and break up after an infidelity crisis assume that they won't have any regrets. Yet I can tell you from professional experience that isn't always the case.

Although I have for years been in the business of saving marriages and helping couples keep their families together, I took a somewhat backward route to this career path.

I actually began my post-law school career as a divorce mediator. I was in the business of helping marriages and families break apart, albeit as amicably as possible.

The time I spent as a divorce mediator gave me a unique perspective that too few marriage professionals have: it gave me a birds-eye view of what causes a marriage to break down and fail. It also showed me the aftermath of marital and family breakdown.

I'm now something of a relationship "reverse engineer." I know what causes the end product – broken trust and divorce – to happen, and I use that knowledge to help couples rebuild trust and revive the love, devotion and happiness in their marriage.

When I worked as a divorce mediator, I saw how my clients had run their relationships into the ground. How they spoke to each other with contempt, criticism and self-centeredness. How they had made stupid mistakes and how they had stopped showing each other affection, appreciation and adoration.

How they let themselves go, let sex slip off the radar, let resentment fill their hearts, let their kids call the shots, let someone else in their heart or in their bed, let it all slip away.

And how they were now sitting in my office, pretending to be interested in the art on the walls, while really they were scared out of their wits that they were going to lose custody of their kids, ownership of their home, half the assets they had spent years toiling for, the respect of family and friends, a gazillion memories they had made with their spouse and a lifestyle they used to love.

It can be strange to sit in a room with people like this. Not so long ago, they were madly in love with each other. They were laughing at the same things and staying up all night binge-watching their favorite TV show.

Not so long ago, they were intimately sharing their bodies, surprising each other with sweet acts of kindness, and sneaking into the living room together at midnight to put presents under the Christmas tree, fussing over which gifts their kids should see first.

And now they couldn't even stand the sight of each other.

Sometimes, the anger and resentment between them are palpable. But other times, and far more often than you might think, the room is packed with wall-to-wall sadness, fear – and regret.

The air is heavy with emotion, but neither of them has the courage or humility to say the things they both desperately want to hear. *"Are we sure we want to do this? Did we try hard enough? Might there still be some love between us? I am so sorry."*

As I began to pick up on this vibe more and more, I started to change my approach. I would sit back, tuck "the papers" into a folder and say, "We don't have to do this right now. If you want, we can just talk for a while."

And that's exactly what we'd do.

More and more, couples who had booked appointments for divorce mediation were reconnecting right before my eyes. As our sessions proceeded, their voice tones and expressions softened. Their body language opened up. They started making eye contact and talking to each other, rather than just talking through me.

For many of my clients, the time they spent with each other in my office was the first time they had communicated with insight or interacted with purpose, positivity or affection following whatever breach of trust had happened between them.

But we did more than just talk. At some point, talking doesn't cut it (that's why talk therapy and counselling are often counter-productive). I sent spouses home with lists of "do's" and "don'ts" that I wanted them to follow between sessions. Many of them needed that kind of step-by-step direction to navigate their way back to each other, especially after an affair or indiscretion.

Although my initial goal was simply to make these couples get along for the sake of their kids, my unique approach to couples mediation began to spark long-forgotten feelings of friendship and love between them.

This was an emotional process for many couples, especially those who were beginning to realize how poorly they had treated each other and how little they had understood each other.

Armed with this new insight, humility and motivation, some couples began to see the infidelity in their relationship as almost inevitable.

Before I knew it, new clients were phoning me up and – instead of asking for divorce mediation – were asking whether I could help them move past infidelity and other indiscretions, thereby saving their marriages.

Word of mouth had spread that I was offering a practical, no-nonsense and counselling-free way for couples to reconnect and resolve their problems. That was something people wanted.

Eventually, I went with the flow and changed the focus of my private practice from divorce mediation to couples' reconciliatory mediation. That is, I began to help couples save and improve their marriages, and keep their families together.

I particularly began to see individuals and couples whose marriages were at a crisis point – which almost always meant they were dealing with an affair, indiscretion or opposite-sex friendship. Indeed, it was this urgent rescue approach that inspired me to call my private practice Marriage SOS.

Rebuilding trust and a relationship is almost always better than letting it break apart. I've seen couples who were at divorce's door turn their marriages around and become true lovebirds.

I've seen them go on to make years of happy memories with each other and with their kids, puffing up with pride when they talk about the obstacles they've overcome and the life they've built.

Broken trust, in whatever form you're experiencing it, is a painful thing. It will take work to heal, but it can be done. And in the end, getting past it may be better than giving up.

First Things First: Affairs, Sexting, Opposite-Sex Friendships…When Is It Actually Cheating?

Ah, that's a good question. It's an emotional question too, and a person's answer may be influenced by their experience: are they the one who is accused of cheating or are they the one who feels cheated on? What are the circumstances of the situation?

Sometimes the answer to "Is it cheating?" is obvious, as when a wife is caught in bed with another man. It is likely that both she and her husband are going to agree that she has cheated.

At other times, partners may disagree. A spouse who has a very close friendship with an opposite-sex friend may not see it as cheating because they haven't had sex; however, his or her spouse may feel this emotional friendship is more hurtful and frightening, more of a betrayal, than a sexual affair or one-night stand would be.

The question of what constitutes cheating becomes even more complicated and open to debate when we look at online indiscretions and activities.

A husband who has been creating fake profiles on a dating site may say it isn't cheating because there wasn't any physical or emotional aspect. He was just engaging in sex chat with strangers.

His wife might not see it this way. To her, it's cheating. After all, he wouldn't do it if she were looking over his shoulder, right? And since he tried to cover his tracks, he knew it was wrong. Nonetheless, her husband doesn't agree and that makes her feel even more betrayed, angry and hurt.

While the question "Is it cheating?" is a reasonable one, the process of answering it – that is, of having both partners agree on the answer – is a process that can sabotage a couple's efforts to rebuild the relationship before those efforts can even begin.

Why? Because a partner who feels betrayed wants to be validated. She wants her partner to acknowledge the wrong, to admit the hurt he has caused, and to understand how profoundly his actions have wounded her.

She wants him to recommit to her and to comprehend how serious the situation is so that she can begin to trust him again. If he doesn't think it was cheating, then he might do it again. And if he does it again, she has to go through the pain again.

At the same time, the partner who has been accused of cheating may want to downplay the situation, fearing it will spiral out of control if he admits to outright cheating.

He may be embarrassed, regretful and desperate to spare his partner's feelings. He might even truly believe that his actions did not constitute cheating and so – on principle – will deny he did anything wrong.

This type of deadlock happens all the time. And when it does, it is impossible to take even the first steps toward rebuilding trust.

When the definition of what constitutes cheating takes more energy and becomes more important than actually repairing the relationship, it's game-over for most marriages.

Instead of moralizing, dissecting the details of the transgression or arguing over semantics (i.e. Was it an affair, an indiscretion, or just a stupid mistake?) my advice is to think about your goal. Do you want to win some kind of definition award or do you want to move forward in your relationship?

If your goal is to move forward and see whether your relationship can be saved, I suggest agreeing on the term "broken trust." This encompasses a wide range of behaviors and circumstances.

It also describes a situation that neither spouse can reasonably disagree with – that is, at least one of them is struggling to trust the other, for whatever reason.

Finally, using the term "broken trust" allows a couple to label their problem with a term that isn't as ugly or blame-focused as "cheating." It lets them focus on the problem, not the person.

Is it a perfect solution? Nope. When it comes to broken trust, there are no perfect solutions.

Couples must work within the parameters of their own personalities, values, emotions and circumstances to make the best of a bad situation.

What Makes This Book Unique?

This book differs from most infidelity guides in a few ways. First, it has an innovative two-part structure. **Part I is for the partner whose trust has been broken, while Part II is for the partner who has broken trust. This leading-edge approach is the fastest and lowest-conflict way to rebuild trust and affection.**

Each part includes precise advice tailored to the needs, perspectives, emotions and so on of each partner. This is infinitely more useful than forcing both partners to wade through countless anecdotes and filler exercises, each of them trying to figure out what is relevant and who should do what.

Second, this book doesn't contain speculative psychological theories. It doesn't pretend to "diagnose" a problem or a partner. Rather, it is based on my experience as an in-the-trenches couples mediator and marriage expert. **It provides practical strategies and insight – including step-by-step advice – to help couples rebuild trust and make the marriage a happier one for both partners.**

Couples who are struggling with infidelity will have to do some serious soul-searching and answer some tough questions; however, this book tackles these questions without delving into hypothetical psychological disorders or childhood trauma.

Why? Because most cases of broken trust do not stem from psychological illness or past trauma, and launching into unnecessary and unprovable theories only complicates matters. If serious psychological issues are present, it is better to seek in-person help from a mental health practitioner than to rely on a self-help book.

Third, I believe that actions speak louder than words. As such, this book focuses more on "doing" than on "talking." Many spouses – especially men – find this to be a refreshing approach. That's important, since this has to work for both partners.

While I have included tools to help couples have insightful heart-to-heart conversations, many couples find that excessively "talking about it" keeps the painful memory and accusation alive and prevents them from moving forward toward happiness.

That's why many couples stop attending talk therapy. It's like beating the proverbial dead horse. Couples who are in crisis need to move forward, not spin their wheels.

Talking about it is necessary; however, there comes a time when actions have to take over. If that doesn't happen, couples begin to feel hopeless about their relationship. For that reason, this book offers real-world strategies, not psycho-babble. These strategies are meant to start working now, not months from now.

Finally, you'll find that the tone in this book is no-nonsense, with little emotional pandering. My job is to help you save your relationship, not make you feel warm and fuzzy inside. Frankly, I've seen too many "professionals" do nothing more than offer sympathetic nods and empty reassurance. Couples in crisis need more than a soft tissue to dry their tears. They need the hardline.

How To Use This Book "As Allies"

Part I of this book shows a spouse whose trust has been broken how to emotionally cope with an infidelity crisis, gain understanding of the situation and take steps to rebuild trust while strengthening the overall marriage.

Part II shows a spouse who has broken his or her partner's trust how to better understand the situation, wade through emotions and take practical, positive steps to rebuild trust and improve the marriage as a whole.

The goal of this two-part approach is to have spouses working together, as allies, to move past their problems and resolve this crisis in a low-conflict, respectful and positive way.

For this to happen, both spouses will have to do their respective part.

Moreover, the focus has to be on finding and then strengthening the marriage's weak spots as opposed to blaming, complaining or punishing someone for a mistake.

Moving forward, both partners must be happy in the marriage and both partners must have their needs met.

The alliance we are forming here will in some ways be a new one that ushers in an age of greater love, happiness, friendship and devotion between you.

Should partners read each other's respective parts? I'd advise against it. There is content that is necessarily redundant in both parts and there's no point reading it twice.

More importantly, focusing only on your part avoids unnecessary conflict and misunderstandings that can happen when you read content that wasn't written for you, and that might hit your emotional triggers.

Here's what I *don't* want to happen: I don't want an angry wife to read her husband's part and then say, "Hey, the book tells you to do such-and-such...why haven't you done it? You aren't serious about this! You expect me to do all the work!"

I don't want this to happen, either: I don't want a defensive husband to read something in his wife's part and then say, "If you think I'm going to do such-and-such, you can forget it!"

To avoid this kind of thing, my advice is that you only read the part that pertains to you. If your partner is motivated and committed to repairing the marriage, he or she will read and do his or her part. Accepting that fact is the first step to rebuilding trust.

Plus, you have your own work to do. Whether you are the partner who broke trust in the marriage or the partner whose trust was broken, there is absolutely no doubt that you will have to make some changes to your behavior and outlook if you want to rebuild that trust and have a stronger, happier marriage moving forward.

As I've said, you may dislike some of the changes you'll have to make. Depending on your circumstances, personality or personal desires, you might even see them as sacrifices or unfair demands.

For example, some unfaithful spouses have been living by their own rules for a long time and may resist change.   At the same time, some betrayed spouses assume that, on principle, they shouldn't have to make any changes or exert any effort.

That's where those qualities of love, maturity, humility, perspective and motivation come in. If you want have a marriage where both spouses are happy, you'll both have to do the work.

Otherwise, you might as well choose to divorce and spare yourself, your spouse and your kids the grief that comes with a half-hearted attempt to rebuild trust and save a marriage. From what I've seen over the years, an insincere or self-focused attempt to save a marriage is far worse than no attempt at all.

A final note: Throughout this book, you will see the words "wife" and "husband," as well as gendered pronouns (i.e. he/she, his/hers, him/her) used interchangeably.

The purpose is to facilitate easy reading, not imply that one sex cheats more. I see about equal rates of male/female infidelity in my private practice.

You will also see the words "marriage" and "relationship" and "spouse" and "partner" used interchangeably.

This book is intended for all committed couples, whether married, common-law, cohabiting or dating. The issues presented herein are relevant to all couples who are trying to rebuild trust and make a better life.

How To Use This Book Alone:
When Your Partner Won't Participate

Although this book is ideally used by both partners, it can be very successfully used by a partner who wishes to take the lead and save the marriage or relationship.

It may be that you have broken your partner's trust and he or she is simply too angry, hurt or apathetic at this point to participate in the process. That's fair enough. The worst thing you can do is try to persuade or guilt your partner into doing something he or she isn't ready to do. This will only backfire.

If the actual betrayal was on your part, it is unwise and counter-productive to now say, *"I'm willing to work on our marriage, but obviously you aren't!"*

I suggest you read Part II and do everything therein without your partner asking. Show him or her that you have the humility to take the lead and that you aren't just "all talk."

Part II will walk you through the real-world steps you can take to show your partner that you are serious about regaining his or her trust. Actions speak louder than words.

This part of the book will also help you gain essential insight into how your partner is feeling, and how you can manage his or her intense emotions, meltdowns, accusations, demands and so on.

Finally, Part II can help you gain some insight into why the infidelity or indiscretion happened. This is necessary, since your partner will want some kind of explanation. The absolute worst thing you can say is, *"I don't know."*

The more you can follow the instructions in Part II, the more likely it is that your partner will realize you are sincere in your attempts to rebuild trust and save the relationship. This can motivate him or her to step up and begin to participate.

In some cases, it is the unfaithful partner who refuses to participate. It may be that your partner is embarrassed or angry at being "busted" or that he or she has been unhappy in the marriage for some time and won't end the extramarital relationship.

In a very common scenario, it may be that your partner is having an opposite-sex friendship that he or she doesn't believe is inappropriate, or that is actually an early emotional affair. Such a partner may refuse to end that friendship.

My advice is to read Part I. It offers great insight into the heart and mind of an unfaithful spouse, and that is information you need to know. It also provides vital information to betrayed spouses so that they can take steps that are in their best interests.

Part I also offers real-world strategies that can motivate an unfaithful partner to end an extramarital relationship – including an opposite-sex friendship – and focus on the marriage instead.

Part I

To Be Read By The Spouse Whose Trust Was Broken

Getting Through The Day

Let me guess: Your emotions are all over the map, right? One moment you're angry, the next you're heart-broken, the next you're confused, the next you're terrified...and so on. Take a deep breath. Feel your body relax and your mind clear. Let your emotions settle out. It's hard, but try to do it.

We have some heavy stuff to talk about. As we do, I want you to keep something in mind: While you are experiencing a relationship crisis, this is not a true "emergency." Your house isn't on fire. You aren't falling off a cliff, even if it feels like it.

You don't need to make any big decisions right now. You don't need to decide whether to stay or go. You don't need to decide whether you'll ever be able to trust your spouse again, have sex with him or her again, or even look at him or her without breaking into anger or tears.

For right now, it's one step at a time.

Despite the turmoil of this time, your life has to go on. You have to get up in the morning, be there for your children, remember to feed the dog, go to work, pay the bills...you get it.

It might feel like the bottom has dropped out from under you, but – and I don't say this lightly – you still have to find a way to get through the day.

A spouse who has been betrayed must learn, to some extent, to put her anger, shock, sadness, confusion and fear on an "emotional shelf" so that life can go on and she can function.

To do this, remember that this infidelity doesn't define your life or your marriage. You're more than a person who has been betrayed and your spouse is more than a betrayer. As hard as it is, it is essential to have this kind of perspective.

Taking care of yourself physically and emotionally should be a priority. Eat well. Exercise. Take long, hot baths and a read a good book that can help distract you, even for a little while, from the turmoil. Write down your thoughts and feelings in a journal.

Tinker in the garage or turn to your favorite hobbies. Take your kids to the movie and listen to music. Try to find relief through laughter when possible.

None of this is meant to trivialize your feelings. It's only meant to encourage you to slow down your thoughts and soothe your emotions to the extent that you can.

Recovering from infidelity doesn't happen overnight. It's a long process and you will have to learn to exist through the sadness, shock, anger or fear.

The good news is, the initial shock does wear off. The emotions, although still intense and unpredictable, become more manageable.

Many people who have been betrayed long to feel comforted by the very person who hurt them – their spouse. I've had many clients ask, "Is it okay for me to turn to my spouse for comfort? I want to feel his/her arms around me…yet I'm still so angry!"

If you're struggling with that question, you know how confusing those emotions can be. It's natural that you want to feel comforted by your spouse. There is still much love between you.

Before I answer the question, "Is it okay for me to turn to my spouse for comfort?" I want to cover a few important things that will determine whether that answer is Yes or No.

Technology & Temptation

A few decades ago, infidelity was comparably straightforward: there were sexual affairs, one-night-stands and emotional affairs. It could be tricky to start an affair, too.

First of all, you'd have to "make the moves" in person, risking whether or not the object of your desire would be game to play along.

You might find yourself having to call the person's home and risk an angry spouse answering the phone with, "Who the hell is this? And why do you want to talk to my wife/husband?" This could make it a challenge to arrange meet-ups.

All of that changed with the rise of personal technology (smartphones, tablets, computers) and social media. Now, it is relatively easy and risk-free to toy with infidelity.

All you have to do is send a winking emoticon or innocent "hi how r u?" text to someone and see whether he or she takes the bait. Or even better, you might receive that text and think, "Hey, this is kind of exciting. It can't hurt to play along for a while."

Text messages that begin as "innocent" exchanges between opposite-sex friends or acquaintances are notorious for escalating, at the speed of light, to deeply intimate and sexually explicit conversations. Countless infidelities and indiscretions start this way.

The medium of text messaging provides a false sense of intimacy and friendship that people, especially those who might be a little bored or unhappy in their marriage, quickly over-value. They become preoccupied with the illusion of the relationship and the sexual thrill of it all.

Such pseudo-relationships are easy to carry on, too. Just change the password on your smartphone or computer and remember to delete the conversations, and you're good.

In fact, you can even carry on an inappropriate conversation with another person at your own kitchen table, with your spouse and children only an arm's length away.

If your spouse asks who you're texting, that's easy – just accuse her or him of being paranoid or controlling, and tell her or him that it's private.

Social media sites are similarly tempting and facilitate infidelity. It's all too easy for a spouse to contact or be contacted by a past lover or partner and to find that a few initial innocent exchanges have ramped up into intimate conversation.

Again, this medium fools people into believing that they have connected on a deep, meaningful level with this other person. There is a strong fantasy element at play.

After all, you never see this person at their worst – first thing in the morning, yelling at their kids, feeling sick or grumpy – you just assume they are always as fresh, exciting and positive as they come across on the screen.

But what if you want to have that sense of sexual excitement without connecting with a "real" person in your life?

Well, the Internet has that solved, too. There are countless dating, hook-up and "friend finder" websites and apps that facilitate anonymous sexual connections and conversations.

In only a matter of minutes, a person can create a fake online profile and engage in the type of sexually explicit dialogue that would make a sailor blush.

Whether these exchanges remain anonymous and voyeuristic or whether they progress into in-person meetings is anyone's call. Either way, it stays private.

Or does it? Here's the thing about technology – nothing is ever private. One way or another, many people who engage in this kind of behavior get caught.

They forget to lock their smartphone. They forget to log-out of a site. They leave some kind of trail that their spouse is eventually going to discover, whether by complete accident or because they were suspicious and went digging for it.

Does any of this sound familiar to you? Maybe.

Or maybe not. Maybe your situation doesn't involve the use of technology. When it comes to infidelity, there are many ways to have your trust shattered and your heart broken.

Face The Facts: What You Need To Know

It could be that your spouse has been having a long-term affair with a neighbor, friend or co-worker, or that he or she had a one-time sexual encounter with this person. It may be that your partner has been visiting escorts or paying for sex.

It may be that your partner has been carrying on an inappropriate friendship via text messages, social media or in-person. It could be that your partner has been communicating on various sex-chat websites. It could be almost anything.

Regardless, you need to do some initial fact-finding:

- Who has my partner been seeing or talking to?

- What form did the breach of trust take?

Was it:

    a) Sexual

    b) Emotional

    c) Tech-based

    d) A combination of these

- How did it start and how long has it been going on?

- If they met in person, where and how often?

- How did they or how do they communicate?

- Is it over or still going on?

Emotional chaos often ensues immediately after a spouse has discovered a partner's infidelity. Gathering these basic facts can help a betrayed spouse find initial footing by understanding, at least to some extent, what he or he is dealing with.

Ask your partner these questions in a straightforward way, and ask for straightforward, honest answers. Will your partner answer honestly? Hopefully. If not, the honesty might come as the initial shock of being "found out" wears off and your spouse realizes that despite the betrayal you are willing to work together to get through this crisis.

Once you know these initial answers – who, what, how long, where, etc. – you can begin to think about what else needs to be done. For example, if your spouse has had sex with someone else, you may wish to insist he or she get tested for sexually-transmitted disease. You should do the same.

Knowing the identity of the person your spouse has been seeing or talking to is also important so that you can ensure contact between them stops or is limited to necessary or unavoidable situations (i.e. business) only.

Similarly, you must know how your spouse and this other person communicated so that all forms of communication can be stopped. More often than not, they will have communicated through phone calls, text messaging, email and/or social media. With very rare exceptions (i.e. a co-worker situation), all communication between the two of them must end, immediately.

Ending Contact: Make Sure It's Over

Once you have determined that your spouse has broken your trust, you must ask him or her to end all contact with the other person. It is impossible to rebuild trust or heal a marriage while one spouse is emotionally or physically involved with another person.

Below is a checklist of actions you may wish to request from your partner. Keep in mind, however, that every situation is unique.

Some of these things may not be necessary, relevant or doable in your particular situation. And depending on your preferences, you might not even want your partner to do all of these things.

• Ask your partner to call, text message or email the other person to say that the extramarital relationship is over and he or she is rebuilding his or her marriage. No further contact will be made.

• Ask your partner to delete the other person's contact information and block that person's phone number / email.

• If necessary, ask your partner to get a new phone number or change his or her email address.

• If necessary, ask your partner to delete or suspend social media and other online accounts (i.e. dating profiles).

• If necessary, ask your partner to arrange his or her business affairs to limit contact with the other person.

Again, not all of these actions may be necessary in your particular situation. For example, if your partner had a one-night stand with a stranger, asking him or her to send a "stop contacting me" text is unnecessary and probably impossible.

Even if your partner was having an affair, you may not feel compelled to ask him or her to send a "stop contacting me" text. Your partner's assurances that the extramarital relationship is over, and that no further contact will be made, may be enough for you.

You must strike a delicate balance. On one hand, you need to be sure that the extramarital relationship is over and that contact between your spouse and the other person has stopped.

On the other hand, you don't want to put unnecessarily onerous or humiliating demands on your partner. Ask only for what is necessary.

"What If My Partner Won't End It?"

Here's where it gets tricky. Sometimes, a spouse who has been having an extramarital relationship will resist, perhaps even outright refuse, to end that relationship.

Why? For any number of reasons. It may be that he or she doesn't believe the relationship is inappropriate and wants to continue with the friendship.

A wife who has been texting a male friend and using him as a "shoulder to cry on" may say that the relationship isn't sexual and that her husband is being "controlling" or "jealous" by insisting that she end the friendship (more on inappropriate friendships, below).

It may be that ending the relationship – especially if the spouse considers it an innocent friendship – will cause an inconvenience in matters of business or socializing.

Or it could be more serious. A husband who has been seeing another woman for a while may have feelings for her. These feelings, combined with the ambivalence he may feel toward his marriage, makes him hesitant to end the extramarital relationship.

He is unsure whether his marriage can be saved and he doesn't want to risk losing his affair partner. This husband may say that he "needs more time to think about it," or that he is "unsure of his feelings."

It may also be that the affair is – to put it bluntly – a lot of fun. The truth is, people are people. We don't like to stop doing something that we find pleasure or excitement in.

In some instances, a spouse will hesitate to end an affair because he or she finds it pleasurable to be "fought over" by two people, especially if those people are doing their best to sexually and emotionally gratify him or her in an effort to "win" him or her from the other person.

Regardless, it is my professional opinion that a married couple cannot begin to rebuild trust or work on their marriage while a spouse is involved, sexually or emotionally, with another person.

I take the hardline here. If a spouse is not willing to end an extramarital relationship and cease contact with the other person, an immediate separation is warranted.

Some infidelity self-help books and marriage experts don't agree. They feel that continuing contact may be permissible, even wise, in some circumstances and may say that patience is warranted as an affair "runs its course."

Ultimately, you must keep your own counsel, consider the consequences of any action or inaction you choose, and decide what is right for you.

Nonetheless, I will outline why I believe the extramarital relationship must immediately end.

First, an unfaithful spouse who continues to have contact with the other person leaves his or her spouse in a constant state of emotional turmoil.

The betrayed spouse is often left with an excruciating level of uncertainty, speculation and powerlessness that can seriously compound the heartbreak he or she is already experiencing, and make day to day life almost unbearable.

Every time an unfaithful wife leaves the room with her cell phone in hand, a betrayed husband is left to wonder: *Did he call or text her? Did she call or text him? What are they saying to each other? Are they arranging a time to meet?*

Every time an unfaithful husband is late coming from work or doesn't answer his phone, a betrayed wife is left to wonder: *Is he with her? Are they having sex right now? What is she saying to him about me? What is he saying to her about me or our marriage?*

Few people are equipped to cope with this ongoing level of uncertainty and speculation. Depression and anxiety can be present during an infidelity crisis, and a spouse who knows that the extramarital affair is still continuing is even more at risk.

This can take a toll on a person's emotional and physical well-being, as well as as his or her parenting ability. It's hard to "be there" for your children or to perform well at work when a person feels this powerless, and when so much of his or her energy, emotion and thought are focused on one thing: *What is happening!?*

The second reason I believe that an extramarital relationship and contact must immediately end is because too often the hesitation and indecision on the unfaithful spouse's part – *Which person should I choose? I'm not ready to end it, I need more time!* – become a way of life.

It becomes a permanent and strangely normalized state of indecision wherein the unfaithful partner continues to enjoy the relative safety and pleasure of both relationship options, while the betrayed spouse continues to experience emotional turmoil.

The third reason I believe the affair and contact must immediately end is because allowing it to continue may have lasting negative consequences regardless of the outcome or which relationship the unfaithful partner ultimately chooses.

The following scenario might help illustrate this.

Keith has been having a sexual and emotional affair with a woman for six months. His wife Tracy discovers the affair and insists that he end it; however, he refuses.

He says he has been unhappy in the marriage for a while and, even though Tracy has committed to working on the marriage and being accountable for her own part in their unhappiness, Keith is unsure whether the marriage can be saved. He doesn't want to risk giving up the affair.

He tells Tracy that he "needs time to think about it" and that he "isn't sure of his feelings." Although Tracy wants him to end the affair, she is afraid that if she gives him an ultimatum – "Choose her or me, now!" – he will choose the other woman and the marriage will be over.

Possible outcome # 1: Tracy allows him to continue with the affair, hoping it will "run its course" and he will realize he loves her more. Meanwhile, Keith's mistress is doing her very best to win and keep his heart, so that Tracy feels she must "compete" to keep her own husband.

Eventually, the affair ends. Tracy feels a sense of victory and relief; however, she is never really sure who ended it – did Keith end it or did his mistress end it? She begins to wonder whether she was Keith's "second choice" and whether the affair might start again if the same (or a different) woman reaches out to him again.

After all, Keith now knows that he can carry on an extramarital affair without fear of losing his wife. She must now live with this uncertainty in her marriage.

As time goes on, Tracy's initial sense of "winning" her husband back begins to fade as normal life takes over. She begins to think about how long it took Keith to decide between her and his mistress.

Feelings of anger, indignation, humiliation and resentment begin to take root. She begins to think that all she "won" was an unfaithful husband who regarded her as a "back up plan." Within a few months, the marriage has fallen back into conflict.

Possible outcome # 2: Tracy allows him to continue with the affair, hoping it will "run its course" and he will realize he loves her more than the other woman. Meanwhile, Keith's mistress is doing her very best to win and keep his heart, so that Tracy feels she must "compete" to keep her own husband.

Eventually, Keith decides to be with his mistress and ends his marriage to Tracy. She is shattered. Not only has she lost her husband, but she has lost her dignity as she thinks back on the weeks and months that she stayed in the marriage and in the home, waiting for him to turn to her instead of his mistress.

In this particular scenario, Tracy's decision to stay in the marriage while her husband essentially "chooses" between her and another woman is a decision that is based largely on shock and fear.

She is deeply fearful that if she forces him to choose, he will choose the other woman; however, as the above outcomes show, it is likely that allowing him to continue in the affair will have negative consequences regardless of which relationship he ultimately chooses. For her, sooner or later, it becomes a no-win situation.

For these various reasons, I don't believe it's wise to stay in a marriage where one spouse is sexually or emotionally involved with another person. Doing so – perhaps out of shock or fear – may keep the marriage together in the short term.

In the long term, however, it may be a strategy that just causes a different set of problems and delays divorce while obliterating your dignity in the process.

But back to the matter at hand: What if your spouse refuses to end the affair? In such situations, a separation is warranted. This may have to be tailored to the particulars of your situation and lifestyle. Ideally, one spouse will move out of the home; however, this may not be doable when children are involved or when finances don't allow it.

If that is the case, you may wish to send a strong message by seeing a lawyer about divorce. You may want to talk to the lawyer about protecting your financial interests in particular. Spouses should no longer share a bedroom and relations should be civil (especially if you share children) but not affectionate.

For all intents and purposes, you should act as though the marital relationship is over, effective immediately. Talk to your spouse about how you will handle chores and domestic duties while you are "living together but apart" to minimize disruption and misunderstandings, again especially when kids are involved.

Conversation and interactions should be kept to a minimum. Do not ask your spouse about his or her day. Do not comfort him or her or continue to ask questions about the status of his or her relationship with the other person.

Might this lead to more emotional distance between you and drive your spouse into the arms of the other person? Possibly, yes. That's why it is vital to think through the consequences and choose the course of action or inaction that is right for you.

I only encourage you to think through the long-term consequences of your decision. This can help you decide what will be in your best interests down the road.

If you make a decision to let your spouse continue with the emotional or sexual affair while remaining married to you, what will this do to your sense of dignity and emotional well-being, regardless of whether he or she chooses you or the other person?

Even if your spouse chooses you, will you be able to trust him or her again? Will you ultimately wonder whether he or she secretly wants to be with the other person? Will you wonder whether the affair may start again? What effects will your spouse's indecision have on your marital relationship down the road?

When The Affair Continues: Ultimatums vs. Timelines

Nonetheless, there will be times when a spouse feels that letting his or her partner continue with the affair is the best choice. Why? It may be that the marriage has been an unhappy one for a very long time, and the betrayed spouse doesn't really "blame" his or her partner for finding emotional or physical comfort elsewhere.

For example, a husband who has withheld support, affection or kindness from his wife may quickly realize his role in the problem. He may understand why his wife turned to another man.

He may understand that the ugliness of his past behavior makes it unlikely that his wife will return to him without seeing positive, consistent changes, and he may be willing to do whatever it takes to give his marriage and family a second chance.

In a case like this, he is probably making the right decision to actively work on his marriage and hope the affair will end.

At the same time, a wife who has withheld appreciation and physical affection from her husband may understand why he was drawn to another woman.

She may believe that the affair is largely physical and will end once she and her husband re-establish their emotional and sexual bond.

Despite the possible consequences, she sincerely believes this course of action is in her, and her children's, long-term best interests. And she may in fact be correct.

If you decide to remain in the marriage while your spouse continues to see the other person, I would suggest that you put a timeline on this situation.

As I've said earlier, living in a state of ongoing uncertainty and emotional turmoil can take its toll on a person's life, career, parenting ability, health and overall well-being.

While some people can cope with this better than others, setting a timeline can help bring some certainty to an otherwise completely uncertain situation.

But what should that timeline be? One month? Six months? Until the kids are out of school in the summer? Until Valentine's Day, Easter or the New Year?

Sure. Whatever. It doesn't really matter, as long as you know and your spouse knows. Still, I've found that couples who set this timeline around their kids' lives – *"We'll do this until they're out of school at the end of June"* – tend to have better success with sticking to a timeline.

I don't know why. Maybe these "life transition" times have more meaning to us than a random date. Or maybe couples tend to work better when they take their kids into account. Regardless, I just wanted to mention this as I've found it can be helpful.

Although this approach is imperfect, it can still be a reasonable compromise for spouses to agree on; however, an unfaithful spouse who is particularly difficult or belligerent may not see it as a compromise. He or she may see it as an "ultimatum."

Such a person might say, *"So basically you're telling me to make up my mind in a month or you're gone? And what if I'm not ready? What then? As usual, it's all about you."*

Reactions like this may be based in long-term resentment or unhappiness in the marriage. They may also be based in a spouse's desire to remain in the affair indefinitely or at least for as long as possible, while still maintaining the relative comfort and safety of the marital and family life.

It really doesn't matter. As the betrayed spouse, you are entitled to seek the certainty you need to get through the day and to function in your life. You are also entitled to know that at some point you will be able to move ahead with your life, whether that involves rebuilding the marriage or getting a divorce and building a new life altogether.

An unfaithful spouse who views this approach as an "ultimatum," rather than as a reasonable compromise that takes the betrayed spouse's feelings into consideration, shows traits of a highly self-focused person. An unfaithful spouse should have some compassion for the emotional distress his or her spouse is feeling.

If your spouse accuses you of making an ultimatum, it is perhaps best to shrug off the accusation rather than trying to argue. Instead, simply tell him or her that the timeline is there to help both of you get on with your lives.

And leave it at that. If at the end of the timeline your spouse has not made a decision or refuses to make a decision – well, you have your answer.

Why A Betrayed Spouse Should Think Twice About "Competing" With The Other Woman / Man

Keep this in mind: Many people who have extramarital affairs are drawn to the secret, forbidden element of the relationship. The idea of being with the other person is exciting and challenging because that person is in some way unattainable.

And as I said earlier, the situation becomes even more appealing when a spouse feels that two people – the spouse and the girlfriend or boyfriend – are basically "fighting" over him or her.

A spouse who has been betrayed and who feels that she or he must compete for her or his own spouse can dramatically change these dynamics by basically "bowing out" of the competition.

When a betrayed spouse steps back and says, "Go ahead, be together," the other partner's forbidden paramour suddenly becomes fully attainable.

The excitement that accompanies a secret or taboo affair is suddenly deflated. There is nothing and no one standing between the unfaithful spouse and the other person.

Obviously, this is a scary scenario. It is a gamble. It is possible that the unfaithful spouse and the other person will embrace each other; however, it is equally possible that the unfaithful spouse will soon discover that the reality of life with his or her girlfriend or boyfriend doesn't quite live up to the fantasy.

This "bowing out" approach also compels an unfaithful partner to face the situation head-on and made a decision, which prevents him or her from settling into a permanent state of self-indulgence or indecision – *Which person should I choose?* – and subjecting his or her spouse to ongoing emotional turmoil. It allows the betrayed spouse to have control over his or her own life.

Finally, this approach turns the entire situation on its ear by presenting the spouse – not the extramarital partner – as the "unattainable" one.

Instead of finding it a challenge to be with the forbidden person, the spouse now finds it a challenge to be with his or her own spouse.

I've seen this approach make an unfaithful spouse feel suddenly protective of the marriage and possessive of the very spouse he or she betrayed.

You've heard the saying: You don't know what you've got until it's gone. As the betrayed spouse distances herself or himself, the unfaithful spouse must face this truth.

He or she realizes that the spouse is serious and that the love, family life, shared history and so on between them are nearing an end. *"What? You mean I don't get to have my cake and eat it, too?"*

Sometimes, this realization is enough to motivate an unfaithful partner to quickly or immediately end an extramarital affair and strongly re-commit to the marriage.

After all, it's human nature to feel more drawn to someone who is willing to walk away from you than to someone who is begging you to stay.

Again, you must carefully decide for yourself whether this approach is right for you. No one can fault you for choosing another approach. It is your marriage and family life on the line and you must follow your own instincts. If friends or family weigh in with their opinions – *How can you stay with him! Where is your pride?* – ask for their support, not criticism or unsolicited advice.

Frankly, some people are all talk. They might make you feel awful about your decision but, were the same thing to happen to them, it's possible they would act no differently than you.

"Should I Contact The Other Woman / Man?"

Nooooo!!!! Don't do it. Easier said than done, right?

If you don't know who the other woman or man is, you may be painfully curious –*Is the other person more attractive than me? What did my partner see in him or her?*

You may think that confronting them will make them back off or that they might tell you certain details of the affair that your spouse will not reveal.

If you know the other person, you may feel compelled to tell them that you know about the relationship and that their dirty little secret is out. You may want to express your hurt and sense of betrayal and tell them what a terrible human being they are. You may want to scare them by threatening to tell their spouse about the affair.

Some betrayed partners – I'll chalk this one up to shock and not thinking clearly – may even believe that they can appeal to the other person's morality or conscience. *We have a family! Please, let us work through our problems! Please, stop calling my spouse!*

Know this: the other woman or man cannot be trusted or appealed to. They have their own agenda and, whatever that agenda may be, only one thing is for certain: it is **not** to your benefit.

The other woman or man is not a reliable source of information. Nothing this person tells you about the affair can be relied upon as truth.

Getting involved in that person's life by contacting his or her spouse only complicates your situation. You have no idea what is going on in that person's life. His or her spouse may be fully aware of the affair, and may in fact be having his or her own affair. The last thing you need is more drama. You have enough to deal with.

Moreover, when you contact the other woman or man, you send that person a message: You're important. You have a say in all of this. You have some measure of control in my marriage and life.

Ask yourself: Is that the message you want to send the person who has been sexually or emotionally involved with your spouse? Is that the message you want to send your own spouse?

When They Aren't "Just Friends"

Opposite-sex friendships that become too close, too personal, are an epidemic problem in modern marriages. Of course, we all have friends of the opposite sex. The question is one of intimacy.

How intimate is the friendship? Do we discuss our marriage or family problems? Do we offer a shoulder to cry on? Do we find ourselves texting or calling this friend during our personal time, when we should be interacting with our spouse and children? Does our spouse fear or resent the friendship? Do we find ourselves defending the friendship and thus causing marital conflict?

When it comes to the question of when an opposite-sex friendship has become inappropriate, of when it has "crossed the line," there is no cut and dry answer.

Many people can sense when an opposite-sex friendship has become inappropriate. They feel a growing sense of intimacy and familiarity with the other person.

Increasing frequency and intimacy of text messages in particular are a sure sign because, as I've mentioned early, this form of communication creates a false sense of intimacy and affection. And it does so in record time.

But again, people are reluctant to give up an activity or a person that brings them some kind of pleasure. An opposite-sex friendship can bring comfort, support and sexual excitement. It can be fun. It can also tear the heart out of a marriage.

If you feel that your spouse has an inappropriate friendship with another woman or man, the problem should be addressed sooner rather than later. The moment you feel it becoming a threat, you should take steps to prevent it from getting worse.

Your best bet may be to address the issue indirectly at first. If you feel that your partner is spending too much time on his or her cell phone, texting or calling the friend, it may be a good idea to suggest that both of you limit the use of technology at home.

Consider the below scenario.

James and Allison have been married for two years. Their lives are routine: they go to work, come home, surf the Internet on their respective tablets and post updates on social media. Their smartphones are never more than an arm's length away.

Whether they are watching television, doing housework or cooking or eating dinner, they keep their smartphones in-hand and quickly respond to any text messages that arrive from family or friends. Even if they are in the middle of a face-to-face conversation with each other, they will look down at their phones to return a text.

Soon, Allison finds that James is leaving the room to respond to texts. He has also been mentioning a new co-worker – Chloe – quite a bit, and Allison has seen Chloe's name on James's phone. They've definitely been communicating after-hours.

Growing more concerned, Allison checks James's phone one evening when he's in the shower and, sure enough, finds a very personal exchange between James and Chloe. It isn't overtly sexual, but it is more intimate and familiar than Allison is comfortable with.

Fighting the instinct to accuse James of "cheating" or having feelings for another woman, Allison decides to take another approach.

When they both arrive home after work the following day, Allison makes a grand gesture of muting her smartphone and setting it in a kitchen drawer.

She tells James that she thinks she's been spending too much time focused on technology and unimportant people, and wants to spend more time with her husband.

She says that she'd be happy if he would also put his phone away when they get home from work; however, she doesn't insist that he does. Instead, she focuses on him and making him happy.

She asks him to help her cook dinner, and they listen to music and sip wine while they do. She talks about funny times they've shared and they make plans for a summer vacation. She flirts with him throughout dinner.

After dinner, she takes a shower and, to his surprise, asks him to join her, which he happily does. As they dart into bed, he doesn't give a second thought to where his smartphone might be.

You get the idea with this scenario, right? If you can address a situation without attacking or accusing your partner, try that first.

It may be that your spouse is also feeling disconnected and resenting how much time you've been spending on social media or texting people. It is absolutely true that many of us are "addicted" to personal forms of technology like smartphones and the sooner you can break this addiction in your marriage, the better.

In the previous scenario, Allison's approach resolved the problem; however, if your spouse's friendship with the other person is deeper or has been going on longer, it may not be this easy.

It may be that you will have to address the issue head-on. If so, be sure to keep accusation and assumption to a minimum. Instead, tell your spouse that you are feeling disconnected from him or her.

Explain that you feel the emotional intimacy in your marriage is being compromised by the friendship, and that is making you sad and fearful.

Instead of demanding that the relationship end – an approach that may cause your spouse to become defensive and indignant – tell your spouse that you want to be the person that he or she confides in, turns to, talks to, laughs with and so on.

As much as possible, take the focus off the other person and put it on your marriage. Be sure to do this in a positive way, one that conveys a sense of partnership, hope, love and devotion.

If this doesn't work, try the "turn it around" game. That is, put the shoe on the other foot by describing a hypothetical opposite-sex friendship you have developed with a friend or co-worker and then ask your spouse how he or she would feel about it.

As you describe this hypothetical friendship, be sure to give details that add to its impact. *"He calls me every night and I talk to him while I'm in the bath...we talk about you and our marriage problems, and he flatters me and tells me how wonderful I am..."*

As you may unfortunately know, a spouse who finds pleasure in an opposite-sex friendship is often reluctant to let it go. Even if you play the "turn it around" game, it is possible that your spouse will deliberately avoid admitting that the scenario you've presented would bother him or her.

To the above hypothetical friendship scenario, such a spouse might even go so far as to say, *"I'd be fine with that. As long as you weren't having sex, I'd be happy that you had someone to talk to."*

Regardless, you've tried. And you've planted a seed of thought and perspective that, once your spouse has had time to think about it, might make him or her re-think the opposite-sex friendship and the effect it is having on your marriage.

If this doesn't work and your spouse continues to communicate with the other person – and especially if the friendship becomes closer and more time-consuming – you will have to insist that the communication end.

The alternative is to let it continue and become even more entrenched and intimate. Either way, you and your spouse are going to have to deal with this.

Inappropriate opposite-sex friendships are the starting point for emotional and sexual affairs. If you are seriously concerned and nothing has worked, trust your instincts and tell your spouse that you consider the friendship to be an early emotional affair and that you will be treating it as such.

Giving your spouse's relationship with the other person an "emotional affair" label may help impress upon him or her how deeply the situation has affected you, and how much the extramarital relationship is affecting your marriage and life together.

To recap, the below is a workable four-step approach to dealing with an inappropriate opposite-sex friendship in marriage:

1. Approach the issue indirectly by taking the lead and limiting the use of personal technology in your home.

2. Tell your spouse about the disconnection you feel in the marriage, and express your desire to be the person he or she talks to, laughs with, shares things with and so on.

3. Turn it around. Present a hypothetical friendship scenario to your spouse that involves you and another man / woman engaging in a very close friendship.

4. Tell your spouse that you consider the opposite-sex friendship to be compromising the intimacy in your marriage, and therefore to be an early emotional affair.

A final thought here: when asked to end an opposite-sex friendship, many spouses become indignant and refuse. Instead, they turn the situation around by blaming their spouse's insecurity.

They might say, *"You're crazy, we're just friends" or "you're paranoid" or "we just talk about work, get over it!" or "I'm not going to end a friendship just because you're being unreasonable."*

Of course, there are cases where a spouse is particularly insecure, controlling or jealous, or when an innocent text or call is misinterpreted. Yet in my professional experience, most spouses who suspect their partner is having an inappropriate opposite-sex friendship unfortunately have some basis for the suspicion.

Yet it often happens that a spouse who knows in her or his heart that a partner's opposite-sex friendship is inappropriate nonetheless allows it to continue for fear of being labelled "insecure." Nobody wants to feel like a petty, controlling spouse.

If your spouse makes you feel this way or accuses you of being crazy, paranoid, insecure and so on, do not fall into the trap of allowing him or her to turn the tables like this.

Instead of getting into a heated debate about the nature of the friendship, scrolling through miles of text messages to find evidence of wrongdoing or defending or explaining yourself, it is best to let your silence speak for you.

Speak your truth – *"This friendship is inappropriate and I want it to end for the good of our marriage"* – and then do not engage in endless debate. You'll only end up defending yourself and trying, to no avail, to persuade your spouse to see it your way.

It is possible that your spouse knows you're right. In that case, it is better to state your position and then disengage with cool civility. Leave your spouse in the silence of having to face his or her own behavior, knowing full well that you "aren't buying it."

Proceed as if the opposite-sex friendship is an early emotional affair. This may mean taking some big, scary steps such as asking your partner to move into the guest room. But what's your alternative? To let the friendship become *more* intimate?

Fake Dating Profiles, Social Media, Porn & Other Online Indiscretions

As with inappropriate friendships, spouses may disagree over whether an online indiscretion – perhaps a profile on a dating site or sex chat with a stranger – is actual infidelity.

My advice stands: instead of arguing over the definition of cheating, it is more productive to agree that trust has been broken in the marriage.

At the very least, that much consensus is necessary to move forward. It allows the betrayed spouse to feel that his or her concerns are being taken seriously, while simultaneously letting the offending spouse maintain some dignity.

After all, many spouses who get caught "red-handed" engaging in online sexual activity can feel very embarrassed by the whole thing.

It's enough for a spouse to admit the behavior was wrong without feeling unnecessarily humiliated or berated.

As many of us know, the Internet can be extremely habit-forming. It doesn't matter what we're looking up – funny cat videos, movie trailers, useless trivia, celebrity news – it's all too easy to lose ourselves for hours in an Internet "shame spiral" of pointless surfing.

Social media is particularly habit-forming as we feel compelled, for some unknown reason, to know what is happening in the lives of friends and strangers alike, and to tell them what is happening in ours.

Now add the thrill of erotic excitement and instant sexual gratification to this magnetic mix. The allure of going online to engage in sex chat, toy with voyeuristic sexual relations or watch pornography can become even more compelling, compulsive and distracting.

More and more, we are seeing quality research being done into the effects of online addiction, both sexual and non-sexual. This book is not an exhaustive study on the topic. Rather, the goal here will be to identify whether this is a problem in your marriage and to offer some practical ideas to move past it.

For most people, this will be enough; however, if your spouse is truly addicted to online sexual activity, including porn, professional in-person therapy from a mental health practitioner who specializes in this uniquely challenging area may be required to help you resolve this issue, rebuild trust, and repair your marriage.

Some spouses who are engaging in online sexual activity will confess and tell their spouse about it, whether out of sadness, shame, guilt or a realization that a change has to happen.

More often than not, though, an unaware spouse finds his or her spouse's online sexual activity either by accident or by actively looking for it on a smartphone, tablet or computer, most likely motivated by suspicion.

If you have come across this kind of material or activity, do **not** attack your spouse with a barrage of emotion or accusation. Yes, you are hurt. Yes, it may be inappropriate.

But confronting your spouse in anger is most likely going to cause an even angrier reaction as your spouse accuses you of snooping through his or her private accounts and violating his or her privacy in the process. And if that happens, you will spend more time defending yourself than actually working through the issue.

Keep in mind that your spouse will probably feel a mixture of emotion when he or she realizes that the activity has been revealed.

In addition to the anger of having his or her privacy violated and the embarrassment of being found out, your spouse may be struggling with his or her own dissatisfaction in the marriage.

Many spouses – men and women – who are happily married will engage in some extent of online sexual activity, such as occasionally viewing Internet porn or reading online erotica.

In most instances, the activity does not compromise the relationship. In fact, some spouses engage in this as a way to spark arousal for lovemaking. In this way, the activity can enhance or maintain sexual and emotional intimacy. Online sexual activity is present, but the relationship is always prioritized.

However, problems arise when a spouse engages in activity that becomes compulsive or habitual, or that takes time, energy and intimacy away from his or her spouse. The activity is prioritized over the relationship.

Problems also arise when the activity involves interaction with a "real" person, even a stranger. Sex chat, online dating profiles that send and receive messages, and live-streaming, interactive pornography are examples of activities that a spouse may reasonably feel violate the privacy that should exist within marriage.

So how to confront a spouse who is engaging in this type of activity? Well, the first step is to determine how inappropriate the behavior really is. If you feel it is inappropriate, you must be careful to choose the right time and mood to broach the subject.

For example, it is utterly pointless to bring it up during an argument or when emotions are high. Doing so will only add to the negativity and accusations that are flying around.

It is equally counter-productive to wake your partner up from a deep sleep and wave the print-outs you've made of every X-rated conversation you've found in front of his or her face.

Remember something I said near the beginning of this part of the book: this is not an emergency situation. Yes, it is upsetting and shocking and emotional. But you must think long-term and keep your thoughts and feelings focused on your goal – to save your marriage.

Instead, choose a time when you feel you and your spouse are connecting, and that emotions are stable. Begin the conversation by expressing your love and desire for both of you to have a marriage that is happy, strong and respectful.

Tell your partner that you came across something on his or her phone or computer that concerned you, something that made you wonder whether he or she was "satisfied" in the marriage. Something that made you feel unsure about the commitment level in your marriage.

If your partner accuses you of snooping, you may want to admit to it and sincerely apologize, insisting that your motivation was to find out what was wrong in the marriage and fix it. This may defuse the situation – if not initially, at least eventually.

If you truly did discover the activity by accident, you can say so – just don't get into a "yes I did" versus a "no you didn't" match. Try to move the conversation along to more substantial matters as quickly as possible.

Be sure to keep your voice tone calm and non-accusatory. I know this is easier said than done; however, the alternative – to "freak out" and point fingers – isn't going to help matters.

Instead, talk about your shock and sadness. Talk about how you feel fearful for your marriage and partnership, and how you are committed to having a marriage where both spouses are able to turn to each other to have their needs met, rather than going online.

When it comes to moving past an online indiscretion, couples should work together to find solutions that work for both of them.

It may not be realistic to "ban" one spouse from using all forms of personal technology. In fact, that is probably going to be impossible.

Begin by asking your spouse what drew him or her to the online activity. What was compelling about it?

Ask whether the activity was meant to fill a void in the marriage. That is, did it bring an element of sexual variety, excitement or fulfillment that your spouse wasn't getting in the marriage? Was there an emotional element to it?

This might be hard to hear; however, as long as your spouse is being honest and forthcoming, be sure to listen with an open heart and an open mind.

The goal is not to punish, it is to understand and to heal.

At some point – again, when the timing seems right – you should explain to your spouse how his or her online activity impacted you, whether emotionally or sexually or both. Let your spouse know that the behavior, albeit tech-based, was not as "impersonal" as it may have seemed.

Working together, try to identify the triggers that led your spouse to engage in the activity. That is, were there certain emotions or events that prompted him or her to go online to seek some kind of gratification?

This line of questioning can also identify weak spots in the marriage that may have contributed to the behavior.

You will also have to work together to decide, in a practical sense, how to prevent the behavior from recurring and further chipping away at your partnership.

For example, if your spouse's habit was to go downstairs after supper and surf dating or sex sites on his personal computer, you might want to re-structure your lifestyle so that you and your spouse are doing something enjoyable together instead.

Asking your spouse to delete any real or fake profiles he or she has on dating sites is a must. Deleting or suspending social media accounts may also be necessary.

A good way for couples to move past online indiscretions and to enhance a sense of privacy and partnership in the marriage is to create joint social media accounts and personal email addresses.

This can reinforce a couple's sense of identity and send a message to the world that you're a united front. Every time a spouse goes online, he or she is moving about in cyberspace as one half of a two-player team.

Building A Fortress Around Your Marriage

Whether your marriage is struggling with the strain of a full-blown sexual or emotional affair, an online or other indiscretion, or an inappropriate opposite-sex friendship, it is essential that you and your spouse begin to feel "protective" of your marriage.

Strong marriages do have a fortress of sorts around them. In fact, it can be helpful to use this metaphor to discuss privacy in your marriage in a larger sense.

This fortress embraces the couple and any children they have. Its walls keep feelings of love, friendship, devotion and happiness in.

The walls of this fortress also keep destructive forces out. That includes other people who could in some way "chip away" at the marriage, including nosey in-laws, negative family members, judgmental or opposite-sex friends and extramarital partners.

Seeing your marriage in this way can summon positive feelings of protectiveness. It can even change the way a person thinks about an opposite-sex friend or affair partner.

Instead of this person being a friend or confidante, he or she becomes an intruder and an enemy. Instead of defending the extramarital relationship, a spouse feels more compelled to defend the marriage and family unit.

In keeping with this marital fortress of love, devotion, solidarity and privacy, you should be careful and selective when choosing the people you will talk to about the infidelity in your marriage.

Like it or not, your marriage problems may be nothing more than gossip to some of your friends. Your friends and family members may be unduly influenced by their own negative feelings, experiences or agendas and this in turn may influence you.

Ideally, spouses should agree on the friends or family members that they can each turn to as confidantes. You are dealing with enough feelings of betrayal in your marriage. Don't add to them by talking to someone your partner doesn't trust.

Unfortunately, you may have to reveal your personal situation to some people you wouldn't normally confide in. For example, if the infidelity was with a co-worker, your spouse may have to inform a superior to arrange transfer to another department or to otherwise limit contact with the other person.

If the affair was with a family friend, you may have to tell certain other people to ensure that you don't bump into the other person at social events.

Commit To Restoring Trust &
Building A Fortress Around Your Marriage

Okay. You know your partner has broken trust. You know how and with whom. Your partner has ended the relationship with the other person and has restricted contact to only what is absolutely essential or unavoidable. You've told the people who need to know.

You've taken other initial steps, such as re-structuring your online presence, deleting problematic email or online accounts, or suspending or uniting social media accounts.

Now what? Well, now you're ready to really get to work. Now you're ready to rebuild the fortress around your marriage and family, brick by brick, by working as allies and not enemies.

Now you're ready to move on to the more significant steps you must take to move forward, re-establish trust, understand why it all happened and ultimately prevent it from happening again.

Transparency

The fortress around a strong marriage is rock-solid when seen from the outside. No one can see through the walls. It's hard to know what's happening inside.

And that's a good thing since, most of the time, it's no one else's business.

Inside the walls of the fortress, however, the view is crystal clear. Spouses can see everything. There is total transparency. Nothing is hidden. And never is this transparency more important than in the weeks and months following a breach in trust.

Spouses who are struggling to rebuild after infidelity should agree to leave smartphones and computers unlocked and accessible by the other partner.

They should agree to share passwords to all electronics and social media and other online accounts.

It is counter-productive to demand that only the unfaithful spouse provides this level of transparency. Yes, he or she is the one who broke trust; however, if you want to have a strong fortress around your marriage, both spouses have to play by the same rules.

Mutual transparency within marriage is one of the smartest, most practical things you can do to resolve a breach of trust and prevent future breaches from happening.

As a betrayed spouse, you may feel compelled to check your partner's smartphone or computer for "evidence" that he or she is continuing contact with the other person.

In the aftermath of discovering an affair, doing this may help soothe your anxiety and prove that your spouse is doing his or her part. Fair enough.

Just be sure that this doesn't become obsessive or a way to continue to punish your partner. Checking a spouse's phone or computer too often can keep a betrayed spouse in a constant state of fear and suspicion.

It can also become highly irritating to the other spouse, even one who is committed to transparency.

There comes a point where checking your spouse's phone or computer becomes more about habitual behavior than moving forward toward a state of trust where checking these things is unnecessary.

After all, if a person truly wants to hide contact or a communication, he or she will find a way to do that.

At some point you will have to exercise restraint when you see your spouse's smartphone lying on the counter, tempting you to scroll through the text messages and email.

You must know that, in the end, your spouse will choose to be faithful or unfaithful, regardless of how many times you check. Learn to trust yourself and your partner, not an electronic gadget.

Now back to a question that was posed at the beginning of this part of the book: "Is it okay for me to turn to my spouse for comfort? I want to feel his/her arms around me...yet I'm still so angry!"

Here's my take on it: If your spouse has been:

a) honest and forthcoming with the facts of the infidelity

b) has ended the relationship with the other person

c) has ended contact with the other person (where possible)

d) has agreed to transparency

e) has agreed to work with you to build a fortress of privacy, love, respect and devotion around your marriage

...then yes, I think it's okay to seek comfort from that person. In fact, it may be wise and productive to do so since, moving forward, you will be working together, as a team, to rebuild trust and strengthen your marriage.

Indeed, this is the goal of any marriage, not just one that is struggling. The sooner you and your spouse can say, "It's us against the world – we're in this together," the better.

The Gory Details

Richard and Denise had been married for almost twenty years. Their marriage had for the most part been a happy one. Their sex life had also been good, despite the ups and downs and dry spells that come with raising children and reaching middle-age.

Once their kids had grown and left home, Denise quit her job as a hairstylist to start her own business. The business struggled for a few years and the financial stress put a strain on their marriage.

Although he had been initially supportive, Richard began to criticize Denise's business acumen and the viability of her company. The more Richard criticized Denise, the more Tyler – a friend of theirs who had recently went through a divorce – stepped up to support and comfort her.

Denise and Tyler began an emotional affair that soon turned sexual. It continued for several months, until Tyler's ex-wife somehow found out about it and told Richard.

Richard was devastated; however, he knew he had grown cool and unsupportive toward his wife and was willing to admit that. Denise immediately ended the affair and cut all contact with Tyler. She and Richard committed to rebuilding their marriage.

Yet despite the significant progress they made, Richard could not get past the "visual" of his wife in bed with another man. He kept picturing Denise and Tyler making love. He began to ask Denise a constant barrage of questions about the "gory details" of her sexual encounters with Tyler.

"What positions did you do it in? Did you give him oral sex? How many times? How did he touch you? Did you do anything with him that we haven't done? Was he bigger than me? Did he last longer than me? Did you use any toys? Did you look in his eyes when you had an orgasm? Show me how you touched him…"

The questions didn't stop. Worse, they became increasingly explicit as Richard asked about the details of every sexual act.

Although Denise had been committed to rebuilding her marriage, the questions became emotionally exhausting and personally humiliating as she had to "tell all" in gory detail.

Eventually, Denise again began to feel criticized and unsupported by Richard. His questions made it impossible for her to forget the details of the affair and she began to think about it again.

Soon after, Denise and Richard decided to separate.

To be sure, picturing one's spouse having sex with another person is about as gut-wrenching and heart-breaking as it gets. It's also one of the most pointless ways to torture yourself.

A betrayed spouse is entitled to certain information and to know that his or her spouse has a) ended the affair, b) ended contact, and c) will do his or her part to save the marriage (i.e. agreeing to transparency, working through this book).

But not all information is this relevant or helpful. Some information is harmful. Information that keeps a betrayed spouse in a state of heartbreak and anxiety is counter-productive.

Once you've heard something – a gory detail – you can't unhear it. You picture it and then you can't get that picture out of your mind. It becomes an ugly, unpredictable image that can seep into your thoughts even during those times when you and your spouse are happy or making real progress.

Here's the thing: memories fade. Whatever your spouse and the other person did, those memories will fade from his or her mind; however, they will fade faster if you stop reviving them.

They will fade even faster if, instead of reliving them, you replace them with new experiences and memories that involve you and your spouse being happy, loving and ultimately sexual.

"My Spouse Still Isn't Being Honest!"

While this book and most books on infidelity operate under the assumption that both spouses are working together to rebuild trust and save the marriage, many unfaithful spouses will continue to deny, deny, deny, even in the face of evidence that proves the affair beyond a doubt.

Some spouses will come up with all kinds of excuses, some of which would be laughable if they weren't so hurtful. I hope that none of the following look familiar to you.

I didn't send her that text...my buddy sent it from my phone as a joke!

I only sent him that email to test whether you were still checking my computer!

I don't know how that hotel receipt got in my jacket pocket...someone must have put it there by mistake!

Other spouses will fall back on belligerence as a way to defend their dishonesty or, just as bad, to downplay the seriousness of their own actions and bully their spouse into "dropping it."

For Christ's sake, get over it already! I said sorry – what else do you want from me?

Honestly, if you bring it up again, I'm out of here. It was over two months ago. You're turning into a psycho bitch over this. It was nothing. Get off my fucking back.

Still other spouses will try to blame the entire thing on the betrayed partner.

That's what you get for snooping through my phone! If you'd spend more time listening to me, I wouldn't have to talk to him so much!

You knew when you married me that I'm a very sexual person! If I'm not getting it at home, then I'm going to get it somewhere else. What did you expect?

In these instances, the unfaithful partner is not invested in saving the marriage. A spouse who acts like this – with belligerence, name-calling, blame or a short-fuse – feels like any efforts to save the marriage are more trouble than they're worth.

Rebuilding trust and saving a marriage can be very hard work, even when both spouses are completely honest, respectful, committed to the process and highly motivated to stay together.

So you can imagine what a challenge it is to save a marriage when one spouse refuses to participate in a loving, respectful or sincere way, or refuses to abide by promises he or she has made.

Trying to rebuild trust or strengthen a marriage when one spouse is actively and perhaps even belligerently being dishonest or indifferent is like driving on a dead-end road. There's simply nowhere to go. The sooner you begin to travel a different path, the sooner life can take you to happier places.

As much as I hope you can move past infidelity and have a happier, stronger marriage, that doesn't always happen. It only takes one to break trust, but it takes two to rebuild it.

A Return To "Normalcy" In The Home:
From Children to Chores

Once the initial ground-work of rebuilding trust has been done (i.e. the extramarital relationship and contact has ended, you know the essential facts, you've agreed on transparency, etc.) you and your spouse should re-establish some normalcy in the home.

This is especially so if you have children. To them, it should be "business as usual" as soon as possible.

Infidelity is an issue that most adults have great difficulty understanding and coping with – so you can imagine how it affects a child.

While it may be necessary and wise to let your children know that "mom and dad" are facing a challenge, the message should be that you are facing it together, for the most part behind closed doors. As a team. As allies.

Your kids must know that no matter what happens, their parents will continue to be in their lives and will continue to co-parent in a way that shows respect to each other.

As parents, you know your children best. You know their personalities, maturity levels, fears and strengths. You know what they can handle for their age.

Just don't overestimate what they can handle. An older child who asks, "What's wrong, Mom? What can I do?" is doing so out of love, fear and concern.

Do not assume that child is capable of being your confidante or counselor, and do not divulge unpleasant details to them. Do not let your child "parent" you.

Never unload on your children or solicit them to "take your side." They are living with enough stress and uncertainty right now.

At this point, you don't know how this is going to end. Leading your children to resent the other parent can cause serious, lasting damage to the parent-child relationship. It can cause lasting damage to your relationship with your kids too, as they one day look back at your behavior and come to their own conclusions.

Soliciting your children to take your side or telling them your problems can also damage your marriage and family life even if you are able to move past those problems and stay together.

Despite the stress and emotion that descends on a household during a crisis of broken trust, life must go on. You and your spouse should commit to working together to ensure the day-to-day demands of daily life are met.

This can be a challenge when emotions are high. You and/or your spouse may find yourselves becoming quickly irritated, insulted or hurt by even the most innocent or well-meaning of actions or statements. You might be quick to anger, break into tears or jump to negative conclusions.

For example, I've seen couples who were making real progress suddenly lose ground and descend into conflict over something as seemingly insignificant as a sink full of dirty dishes.

I've seen couples who had rebuilt significant trust suddenly fall into fear, suspicion and assumption on account of a dead battery in a cell phone and a check-in phone call that came ten minutes later than a spouse expected it would.

My point is this: you and your spouse should be clear about what you expect of each other in terms of housework, the kids, paying bills, socializing, checking-in with each other and so on.

Do not assume that your spouse will have the same expectations as you. He or she probably won't. This is a time for clear communication and cooperation, not for mind-reading.

Talking About It:
Phase I & Phase II

In my experience, many spouses who discover their spouse has in some way broken the trust in the marriage are too quick to demand that they "talk about it" for hours, days, weeks on end.

Despite the intense anger, sadness, fear and other intense emotions and assumptions that attend infidelity, too many couples launch into this discussion without any kind of structure or plan.

They just start talking. And then guess what? They usually start fighting. It's almost inevitable.

I always recommend a two-phase approach when talking about and coping with infidelity. This helps bring some structure to an otherwise chaotic discussion, and moves the conversation ahead in a purposeful, not emotional or impulsive, way.

Don't underestimate the value of structure and patience. After all, this breach of trust may be the most important thing that you and your partner ever talk about in your lives.

In the immediate aftermath of a discovered infidelity, certain facts need to be known and certain actions need to be taken. This is phase I, the stabilizing phase, and it includes the kinds of things that you've read so far, including:

- The identity of the other person

- Was the infidelity emotional, sexual or tech-based

- Whether the extramarital relationship has ended

- Whether contact between them has ended

- Agreeing on transparency (i.e. shared passwords, etc.)

- Establishing a mutual commitment to work on the marriage and build a fortress of love and privacy around it

- Establishing normalcy in the home by discussing how to deal with the kids, check-in with each other, share housework, etc.

This is how I think of this initial phase: Imagine a gunshot victim being rushed into the emergency room of a hospital. He is in shock and his vital signs are weakening by the moment.

Of course, the bullet needs to be removed. But before the patient has the strength to survive the operation, his condition must be stabilized.

X-rays must be taken to show where the bullet is. Once that happens, he can survive the process – the operation – that must happen if his life is to be saved.

It's the same thing with infidelity. In the wake of an infidelity, both spouses are in shock. The betrayed spouse is in the shock of discovery while the unfaithful spouse is in the shock of being found out.

Before these spouses can survive the process of rebuilding trust and saving their marriage, they must stabilize their life and situation. They must know the basic facts of the matter and arrange their lives in a way that will support them as they move forward.

And again, that's what you've done until this point.

If phase I is the stabilizing phase, then phase II – which is where you are now – is what we can think of as the recovery and prevention phase.

Now, it's time to dig a little deeper. Now it's time to move toward more meaningful heart-to-heart conversations about why the infidelity happened. What made the marriage vulnerable to it? How did each spouse contribute to it? How can a couple make sure it doesn't happen again?

These questions take longer to answer. They require a long-term commitment, self-reflection, humility, great love for our spouse and a willingness to change one's behavior, outlook and perhaps even priorities.

Of course, a couple who is struggling to rebuild trust and strengthen their marriage will have to talk through their problems and pain to find insight and solutions.

That being so, my goal is to make each discussion as purposeful as possible thus reducing the overall number of conversations that are necessary.

Why? Because a couple who keeps talking about it indefinitely, who keeps bringing it up and reliving all the pain that goes with it, will never move past it.

Instead, they will experience regular feelings of anger, betrayal and resentment toward each other, feelings that will eventually settle into a sense of hopelessness about the marriage.

They will begin to think that nothing will ever change. It will never get better. And when couples begin to feel that sense of futility, they tend to "give up."

The Heart-To-Heart: Communication Tips

Let's run through some initial things to keep in mind as you and your spouse begin to engage in heart-to-heart discussions about the infidelity or indiscretion, including why it happened.

• **Timing.** Couples often underestimate the importance of good timing. If your spouse has just walked through the door after a long, unpleasant day at work, it won't be helpful to rush up to him and her and say, "We need to talk right now!" He or she might otherwise be open to the conversation; however, the timing is all wrong and he or she is likely to react with irritation.

Instead, put thought into when you will discuss the issue. In some cases, it is best to schedule a conversation so that spouses can mentally prepare and take steps to limit distractions, such as being interrupted by the kids, phone calls or unexpected visitors.

In other cases, spontaneous conversations can work well, especially if the couple is feeling loving, open-minded and cooperative. Use your own judgment – just think before you speak.

• **Environment.** Arguments and conflict often have a predictable nature to them. Many couples will say that they have the same fight, at the same time, in the place, almost all the time.

To break out of this predictable pattern, think about how you can change your environment so that it contributes to the atmosphere of the conversation in a positive, not negative, way.

I have actually advised some couples to "get away from it all" and spend a night or two in a hotel – even a local one – so that they can talk about their problems against a different background. This in itself can be helpful.

If your partner has a defensive streak and tends to get angry or argumentative whenever you bring up an uncomfortable topic, think about suggesting an evening "walk and talk."

Some unfaithful spouses say they feel "interrogated" or "put on the spot" when asked to talk about their role in conflict. Walking together side-by-side can take the pressure off of a face-to-face communication and make it easier to open up.

You can walk hand-in-hand, moving forward – literally and symbolically – as you have a relaxed heart-to-heart conversation. The invigorating night air, the starry sky and the physical exertion can soothe emotions and keep them in check. This is a great evening ritual to rebuild affection and friendship.

- **Mood.** In addition to timing and environment, it is important to set a "good mood," one that facilitates an honest and positive conversation. Talking by candlelight, playing soft music or even sitting in a hot-tub can all relax the spirit and open the heart.

Humor can help, too. I have suggested that clients watch something funny (i.e. "fail" videos, a favorite comedy or sitcom, etc.) before a serious conversation and to even take "time outs" during that conversation to find solace and perspective in laughter.

The point is not to trivialize the infidelity. The point is to balance a heavy conversation with a lighter tone so that the discussion does not turn into a destructive, hateful one.

A couple who is working through infidelity must learn to tackle all their problems in a way that strengthens, not weakens, the marriage.

● **Your attitude.** No one can blame you for having negative feelings toward your spouse; however, you should try to balance those negative feelings with more positive ones.

To do this, remind yourself that your spouse is willingly participating in the process of rebuilding, even though it is difficult for him or her too. He or she may be embarrassed and emotional.

Remind yourself of the good things your spouse has done for you, for your friends or family, or contributed to your life or home. When we are angry at or hurt by someone, it is easy to forget that person's better qualities and the many ways they have been loving to us in the past.

Try to remember that your spouse is more than just someone who has made this mistake.

● **Positive reinforcement vs. punishment.** As you and your spouse talk through your problems, you will undoubtedly hear things that you don't like. You may disagree with what your partner says at times, or you may feel very hurt by it.

Keep this in mind: If your spouse is being open, honest and respectful of your feelings, he or she is entitled to express his or her complaints about the marriage, even though he or she is the one who broke trust.

Moreover, you *want* your spouse to talk to you. You do not want him or her to shut-down and stop talking. You want to make progress and to do that, you will need to hear him or her out.

Instead of punishing your spouse for what he or she says, show gratitude for your spouse's honesty. By doing so, you set a tone that encourages understanding, collaboration and healing.

• **Voice tone.** Make sure that your voice tone stays positive, pleasant and cooperative. A sarcastic, critical or contemptuous voice tone will sabotage any efforts to move forward.

• **Humility.** We live in a society that is becoming increasingly narcissistic and self-focused. We are very good at expressing our own feelings and complaints, but tend to rise up in defensiveness or indignation when someone else does the same.

Be sure to regularly "self-check" your attitude so that your spouse gets the message that you care about his or her happiness and what he or she has to say.

Spend less time defending yourself or trying to prove how you were "right" and how your spouse was "wrong," and spend more time trying to understand and empathize with your spouse's perspective. That will get you much further.

• **Emotional control.** Not only am I seeing more self-focused clients these days, I'm also seeing more clients who erupt into what can only be described as adult temper-tantrums.

We all lose our cool from time to time and emotional outbursts are to be expected as spouses navigate something as bumpy as infidelity.

Spouses should know their own and each other's "triggers" so they can work together to manage them.

That is, what emotions tend to trigger your and/or your spouse's outbursts? Common emotional triggers include feelings of being unappreciated, unheard, unloved, undesirable, fearful, misunderstood, rejected or not prioritized.

But there's a difference between an occasional meltdown and regular explosions of blind rage, especially if that rage is very easily triggered or accompanied by physically aggressive behavior.

If you or your spouse displays short-fuse or "hair trigger" behavior, and you're unable to control it by yourself or by working as a team, I recommend seeking in-person professional help from a mental health practitioner who specializes in anger management.

• **Emotional oversensitivity.** It isn't just emotional outbursts that can be a barrier to effective communication. Emotional withdrawal or super-sensitivity can also stand in the way.

No one likes to get their feelings hurt; however, a spouse who retreats into wounded silence or bursts into tears whenever their behavior is challenged – even gently so – makes it impossible for their partner to express legitimate complaints.

Self-check yourself for this behavior. If your feelings are "easily bruised" and you are using this to either suppress your partner's complaints or avoid having to answer them in a straightforward manner, you are causing great damage to your relationship. And whether you realize it or not, you are likely causing your partner to feel very resentful toward you.

Just like the person who "blows up" when faced with a criticism, you may succeed in getting your partner to back down and be quiet; however, you're wrong if you think that means the complaints have disappeared. They're still there. They're just bottled up. And inside the bottle, the pressure is growing.

Your partner deserves to have his or her legitimate complaints heard, even if those complaints are hard for you to hear.

If your partner is expressing this behavior, do your best to steer clear of the words that trigger it and always keep a respectful voice tone. Reassure him or her that the purpose of the discussion is to improve the relationship for both of you.

Let your spouse know that you are finding it difficult to say what you need to say, and ask for his or her input – *"What can I do to make the conversation easier for you?"* When he or she does hear you out, show your support and appreciation.

If that doesn't work, you will have to express your own frustrations and feelings of being "controlled" by your partner's oversensitivity. Emotional oversensitivity can be just as controlling and manipulative as emotional outbursts. Some people are fully aware they are doing it, while others haven't considered the impact their oversensitivity has on others.

• **Mind your manners.** In addition to being aware of your voice tone and keeping it respectful, do not interrupt your spouse any more than necessary.

At times it may be necessary to interrupt him or her to clarify something that was said. Just be sure that you aren't interrupting to defend yourself, contradict something your spouse said or to offer unnecessary feedback. People need to feel heard.

Also, watch your body language and ensure it remains respectful and encouraging. Don't roll your eyes, cross your arms in a display of stubbornness or shake your head disapprovingly. The goal is to keep the conversation going, not give someone an excuse to say, "Oh, what's the point? You're not even listening to me."

● **Long-term thinking.** A betrayed spouse often falls into a type of panic mode. There is a sense of urgency: *Tell me everything, now! Are you committed to this marriage? Why did you do it? Talk to me now! How can I ever trust you? We need to fix this, now!*

Yet as I've said earlier, recovering from infidelity and rebuilding a marriage is a long-term process and your thinking should also be focused on the long-term.

There is no magic moment that will mark the end of conflict. There is no magic word your spouse can say that will make you forgive and forget. Instead of seeking a fast, urgent and final solution, it may be wiser to take a more patient approach.

Whether the wound is a physical or emotional one, time does help with the healing process. Instead of seeing time as the enemy, embrace what it has to offer.

"Why Did It Happen?"
Stupid Mistakes, Texting Temptations,
Pre-Existing Problems & More...

Ah, now that's a loaded question and there are countless self-help books, psychological theories and wild speculations as to why trust breaks down in a relationship.

In my professional capacity as a couples mediator, I have seen emotional and sexual affairs, various indiscretions and inappropriate friendships develop for all kinds of reasons.

I'm going to outline a handful of the more common reasons here, and in the subsequent two headings.

Do you see traces of your situation in any of these reasons?

• Sometimes, an unfaithful spouse has suffered some kind of past trauma, was a child of divorce or grew up in a particularly dysfunctional family unit that lacked good role models. These challenges can definitely affect our intimate relationships as adults.

• Other spouses suffer from personality disorders (i.e. narcissism, bi-polarism, etc.) or other challenges (i.e. addiction) which if left unmanaged can make it virtually impossible to enjoy a meaningful, mature and devoted intimate relationship.

• Despite the pain it causes and the betrayal involved, an indiscretion – especially a one-time or minor indiscretion – can be a "stupid mistake." It may have been a temporary lapse in judgment that has nothing to do with a spouse's love for his or her partner or overall commitment level to the relationship and/or family unit.

This can be a difficult – even offensive or insulting – message for a betrayed spouse to hear. After all, how can something that hurt you so profoundly not have an equally profound reason behind it?

It's human nature – when we feel a serious pain, we assume it is caused by something serious. We naturally seek out a reason that is as "big" as our pain.

Normally, that makes sense – the bigger the blade, the deeper the cut, right? But that logic doesn't always apply when it comes to indiscretions.

Have you ever had a paper-cut? They sting like hell, don't they? The pain is great, yet the cut is sometimes so small you can't even see it. No matter how hard you look for the source of the pain, you can't find it.

This isn't meant to suggest that you should dismiss your partner's behavior or shrug it off. Quite the opposite. Your partner has deeply wounded you and must acknowledge that.

Moreover, the two of you must take steps to ensure the behavior doesn't become a pattern in your marriage. Imagine being afflicted with a thousand tiny paper-cuts on your hands.

Even though each individual cut is tiny, the overall pain is excruciating. That's what happens when those "stupid mistakes" start to add up.

• Infidelity and indiscretions may also happen when couples "slide" into marriage after co-habiting or having children. They got married because it seemed like the next step, not because they actively chose to do so.

Such couples are often very much in love; however, the commitment to marriage wasn't there at the time. An infidelity or indiscretion can make these couples re-define their relationship in a more deliberate, clear and committed way.

• Quite commonly, infidelity and other forms of broken trust happen when a spouse feels somehow unsatisfied in the marriage and therefore looks outside of it to find the kind of fulfillment or pleasure that he or she needs.

Ongoing emotional or sexual affairs often fall into this category. A wife who feels unloved or unsupported by her husband might turn to a sympathetic male co-worker who befriends her.

A husband who feels unappreciated and sexually rejected by his wife may turn to a female co-worker who seems to admire him.

This kind of "traditional infidelity" is often believed to be a symptom of an already unhealthy marriage. That is, people tend to have affairs or indiscretions when there are pre-existing problems.

The situation is compounded if spouses don't have the communication or interpersonal skills to understand and resolve their problems before they hit a crisis point. They may exist in a relationship that is fraught with mixed messages, negative assumptions and miserable dynamics.

As you work through this part of the book – and particularly as you get to the Questions To Ask Yourself and Questions To Ask Your Spouse headings – you will find strategies to help you and your partner figure out where any pre-existing problems in your relationship might have been.

- We've covered this before – technology and temptation. More and more, spouses who are in love with and committed to their spouse are being drawn into emotional and sexual affairs, online indiscretions and inappropriate friendships that begin via personal technology. I call these e-affairs or iFriendships.

This type of broken trust is more widespread than you might think and, in my experience, may be becoming the most common type of infidelity that modern couples struggle with.

Since it's unlikely that the growth and development of personal forms of technology is going to slow down, we can expect the rates of tech-based broken trust to continue to rise.

As was covered earlier, personal technology – smartphones, texting, email, social media and so on – make it incredibly easy to get caught up in the "rush" of an emotional or sexual dialogue with another person, whether a friend, a colleague or a stranger.

This creates a false sense of intimacy between a spouse and another person, one that develops into an extramarital relationship far faster than it otherwise would.

Believe it or not, the "traditional" type of infidelity – where a spouse is unfaithful because something is lacking in the marriage – can be easier to remedy. Because there is an identifiable problem, it is easier to identify and agree upon solutions.

In such cases, the betrayed partner is able to see how his or her behavior contributed to the disconnect in the marriage. That can facilitate a spirit of cooperation and help spouses rebuild trust and make their marriage a happier one for both partners. It is easier to work together when both spouses can accept blame.

That can't always happen with today's e-affairs and iFriendships. But that doesn't mean trust cannot be restored and that the marriage cannot move forward stronger and happier than ever.

The truth is, you may never have the perfect explanation of why it happened. You may never be able to write it down in a single sentence, pin it to the wall, point to it and say, "That's why!"

That isn't the end of the world. It doesn't have to be the end of your marriage or relationship, either. There may not be an identifiable answer.

There may be things that your spouse will never tell you. There may be things that are best left alone. You may ultimately choose to focus on the future rather than the past.

When it comes to infidelity, there is no standard approach or prevailing reason. There is no "one size fits all."

There may come a time when you have to work with what you have, with what you know, and make the choice to move forward in good faith.

Did Your Relationship Fall Prey
To A "Partner Predator"?

It isn't always the unfaithful spouse who initiates the infidelity or opposite-sex friendship or who pursues the extramarital person. At times, an otherwise loving and devoted partner can fall prey to what I call "partner predators."

Partner predators find sport in seducing someone else's spouse or partner, and may go to great lengths to do so. They can be masters at exploiting another person's kindness, vanities, weaknesses or personality traits.

Take the classic case of a "lonely, heartbroken" man who seduces another man's wife by playing on her feminine sympathy. He might tell her how his ex-wife cheated on him and how much he wishes he could have met a woman like her instead.

He looks at her with those lovesick puppy-dog eyes until one day he steals a passionate but forbidden kiss. He knows it's wrong and he begs her forgiveness, but he can't help himself! She's just too beautiful and he cannot resist her any longer!

Before you know it, she's swept up in his passion and desire for her and the affair is underway. It's intoxicating. Of course, it's a bunch of bullshit. To him, it's all a game. He's managed to steal another man's wife right out from underneath him, and that's quite the ego boost, isn't it?

Another classic example is the "damsel in distress" who seduces another woman's husband by playing on his masculine desire to feel needed.

She bats her eye-lashes at him and laughs at all his jokes, telling him what a wonderful man he is and how lucky his wife is to have him. Oh, if only she had such a strong, sexy man in her life!

She begins to "rely" on him for more things, until he begins to feel responsible for her. If she isn't asking him to look at her computer or help carry something heavy, she's asking him for his advice about her love life, planting seeds of intimacy.

And then one day as she's crying on his shoulder about how poorly yet another man has treated her, she manages – through her pretty tears – to place a soft, stolen kiss on his lips.

Before you know it, he's swept up in her need and love for him and the affair is underway. It's overwhelming. Of course, it's a bunch of bullshit. To her, it's all a game. She's managed to steal another woman's husband, and that's a real power trip, isn't it?

But what do partner predators do once they've "caught" their prey? That is, what happens when the betrayed spouse ends the marriage, thereby removing all obstacles to the affair?

Well, the partner predator then releases its prey. The thrill of the hunt is gone.

I sometimes compare partner predators to my cat Frosty. Frosty is a very spoiled animal. He has everything he could want; however, he loves the thrill of the hunt and even though his belly is always full, he will hunt mice in the back field and leave them on the doorstep just to prove that he's "still got it."

He never eats these mice. Sometimes he'll gnaw on their tail for a bit, but it's just for show. Once he's caught them, he doesn't want them anymore. He leaves them lying on the doorstep while he trots off, tail in the air, in search of another victim.

So why does he do it? Because it's in his nature. He's a cat. He's a predator.

The ugly truth is, some people are like this, too. Partner predators have nothing to lose in this game; however, they know that their "prey" has everything to lose. And that is part of the fun. That adds to the thrill of the hunt.

There is science to back this up. Research has demonstrated that some people are more attracted to members of the opposite-sex when they know the person is married or otherwise committed.

When told that a certain man or woman is "taken," these predator types experience a pleasurable rush of excitement caused by the brain chemical dopamine.

Dopamine – called the "pleasure and reward" hormone – is produced in increased amounts when a person is "in pursuit" of a potential romantic partner.

Partner predators can become addicted to this rush of pleasure and excitement, motivating them to "catch and release" prey over and over again.

I've seen this play out many times. Sometimes the partner predator will grow bored and leave its prey on the doorstep as soon as something sexual happens. Mission accomplished.

A more vicious species of partner predator will wait until its prey leaves his or her spouse and/or family – believing he or she has found true love – before being satisfied that the hunt is over. It then abandons its prey on the doorstep and sets off on a fresh hunt.

His or her baffled prey – the unfaithful spouse – is left to wonder what the hell happened. *"I thought you loved me?! I risked my marriage for you, and now you're just going to walk away?!"*

This discussion is in no way meant to excuse the actions of an unfaithful spouse. A person who has broken his or her partner's trust is completely responsible for his or her own choices. Don't think for a moment that I'm absolving your partner of his or her accountability or wrongdoing. I'm not.

Rather, this discussion is meant to provide relevant and valuable insight into a scenario that I often see play out when it comes to infidelity. Good people can fall prey to bad people.

Frankly, it's useful to know that partner predators are out there. If you can spot one from a distance, you can work together, as allies, to reinforce and guard the fortress around your marriage and/or family.

I've tried to give Frosty's prey that kind of heads-up. He now wears a flashing neon collar with a bell so that hopefully his prey can see and hear him coming.

Even in the best of marriages and with the strongest of fortresses, partner predators can come sniffing around from time to time. You never when or how they'll strike or which spouse might be the prey. But if you are wise to their "wolf in sheep's clothing" ways, you can chase them away before they go in for the kill.

Was Your Relationship Sabotaged By A "Spouse Scavenger"?

If you'll indulge another animal metaphor, I'd like to briefly tell you about the shady habits of the common cuckoo bird. The common cuckoo is what's called a "brood parasite."

Instead of going through the trouble of building its own nest, the cuckoo waits – watching from a distance – as another pair of birds builds a nest together and the female lays her eggs in it.

Then, when this pair of birds isn't looking, the cuckoo swoops down into their nest, kicks out one of their eggs, and lays its own egg in their nest.

It sabotages, for its own benefit, what the mating pair has already created.

I'm not beating up on the cuckoo bird, here. I wouldn't question the wisdom of Mother Nature. But it is a fairly distasteful tactic, isn't it?

Unfortunately, it sometimes happens that a similar scene plays out within relationships. There are some people who are very drawn to a man or woman who is already taken. Partner predators fall into this category.

So do what I call "spouse scavengers." These people are attracted to those in committed relationships and, like partner predators, can be very manipulative and aggressive when going after what they want.

Yet unlike partner predators – who dispose of their prey once caught – spouse scavengers want to keep what they have found. They want to swoop in and replace the more established spouse/mate.

When I was single, my girlfriends and I used to talk about the qualities we found most attractive in men. Many of us were attracted to the "marrying" type of man. The type of man who was devoted to his wife and family.

Why? Because that type of man has already demonstrated his willingness to commit. The better husband he is to his wife, the better father he is to his own kids, the more we want him to be our husband and the father to our kids. He's a good bet. He displays the qualities we are looking for. I guess it's kind of instinctual.

Unfortunately, some women do more than just talk about their attraction to committed men. Let me walk you through an example.

In my part of the world, oil and gas is the predominant industry and I work with many "oil patch couples."

In a typical arrangement, a husband might be gone for weeks at a time, travelling to various towns and job sites, as his wife stays home to manage the house, the kids and maybe work full or part-time.

Unfortunately, these husbands often catch the eye of single or divorced women who are attracted to the high-income of oil men and the security that comes with it.

One particular case comes to my mind. The husband was regularly sent to work in a small town in the northern part of the province, often spending three weeks out of every month there, while his wife held down the fort at home, many miles away in the southern part of the province. They had two kids, a good marriage and did the best they could to make the situation work.

This particular small town had only one pub. It was the gathering place for many oil workers – and the local women who wanted to snag one.

One of these women, who was also a single mom, was known to flirt with almost every oil man she came across; however, when she met this particular husband, she was particularly smitten.

He was an established supervisor, had a company truck and was the only man on his crew that was married and proud of it. The other guys were either single or divorced, and made it very clear that marriage wasn't on their agenda anytime soon.

The extramarital relationship between them started off slowly. The woman pretended to be interested in a single guy on the husband's crew, which gave her an excuse to befriend him.

She found out his phone number and began to text him, sometimes innocently and sometimes more intimately. She would corner him when he came into the pub alone, and cry on his shoulder about how mean her ex-boyfriend was and how she was in the middle of a battle with him over child-support payments.

One night after a few too many drinks – and assuring him that she had her "tubes tied" and could not get pregnant – she made her big move and they had sex.

Full of remorse and feelings of self-disgust, the husband ended it the next morning. He had himself tested for sexually-transmitted disease and asked his employer to send him to a different job site in the future.

But the deed was done – she was pregnant.

She tried calling and texting to tell him, but he had blocked her phone number. Finally, she called his employer and, impersonating his wife, managed to get through to him on a different job site.

He was shattered. Not only did he have to tell his wife about the extramarital relationship and the breach in trust, he had to tell her about the baby.

It was a brutal revelation; however, he had done everything right in the wake of the infidelity, and those gestures reassured his wife that he was truly remorseful. She decided to stay and work on rebuilding their relationship.

This couple believed that the other woman had deliberately gotten pregnant, most likely so that she could collect the significant child-support payments from the husband.

But the other woman, who already had a four-year-old daughter and another child on the way – didn't just want a monthly check. She wanted the whole package.

She knew he had a big house, two or three vehicles, a boat, a summer cottage at the lake and a nanny for the children. He had the resources to afford the type of lifestyle that she could only dream about. He was her ticket to a fuller, richer "insta-life."

More importantly, he had already demonstrated his willingness to get married, father children and work hard for his wife and family – and that was *exactly* what she wanted and needed in a man.

Her goal was for the husband to divorce his wife and marry her. Her plan was to move into his house as his new wife and step-parent his previous children while they raised their new child together as one big happy blended family.

And she did everything she could to sabotage the now fragile relationship between him and his wife. She did everything she could to shake their nest badly enough that the wife would finally give up and fly away, leaving her to move in.

Although the husband and his wife managed to work through this very serious case of infidelity and stay together, it took a very long time – and eventually a restraining order – for the other woman to abandon her efforts to "supplant" the man's wife.

Is that cuckoo behavior? Maybe. Or maybe in this case, the other woman's efforts were driven as much by economic need and survival as anything else. Regardless, this example does illustrate how the spouse scavenger operates.

While I have in the past typically seen this behavior more on the part of women than men, that is changing. The playing field appears to be leveling out, especially as more single men complain they are having trouble finding "wife material" in the hook-up culture that characterizes today's dating landscape.

I've heard many single men say they feel increasingly drawn toward the stability, lifestyle choices and maternal nature of married women, including those who already have children.

Their assumption is that these married women are somehow more desirable or higher-quality because they've already been "snapped up" by other men. *"If he wanted her that badly, then she must be a real catch!"*

They believe that these women will be able to provide the storybook family life they are looking for, as well as being ideal mothers for their children.

And they believe that, if they play their cards right, they can seduce these women away from their current husbands and family units to set-up their own insta-family arrangement with them.

Again, the scenario I've presented here and this discussion isn't meant to pardon an unfaithful spouse's act of betrayal. It may having absolutely nothing to do with your situation.

It is only meant to provide relevant insight into the complicated dynamics and various agendas that are at play in some cases of infidelity. Partner predators and spouse scavengers are out there and they can wreak havoc on otherwise stable marriages.

The more you can understand why your marital fortress suffered this breach in trust, and the more you can recognize the saboteur tactics used by the person who managed to break through, the more you can work as allies to repair that breach and prevent it from happening again. Knowledge is power.

Questions To Ask Yourself

Most betrayed spouses tend to ask their unfaithful spouse a lot of questions. The biggest question is usually: "Why did you do it?"

We've discussed several common reasons why, from stupid mistakes and personal technology to pre-existing problems and partner predators; however, you will still want to put your own unique situation under the microscope to examine it more closely.

I've heard betrayed spouses say, "The affair came out of nowhere!" Yet once the shock and anger of the initial discovery settles and the focus turns to rebuilding the marriage, betrayed spouses often show some insight into why it happened.

A husband might say, "She's been complaining for years that I don't spend enough time with the kids or family, and that she feels like a single mom."

A wife might say, "He's been complaining for years that I'm negative and that he never feels like he can do anything right."

This kind of self-reflection and insight can help ensure that conversations around the infidelity, indiscretion or inappropriate friendship remain purposeful and productive, rather than descending into nasty sessions of finger-pointing.

For this reason, a betrayed spouse should first ask himself or herself some important questions before simply firing a barrage of angry assumptions and accusations at his or her spouse.

Of course, the unfaithful spouse will have to answer some hard questions; however, the betrayed spouse can help lay a strong foundation for the way they talk about the infidelity as a couple.

I have outlined some questions that you can ask yourself to see whether you can gain any insight into your spouse's behavior.

Remember that the purpose of these questions is to facilitate understanding and collaboration, not to imply that you were to blame for your partner's choices. Even if the marriage had problems, infidelity was not the only option available to him or her.

Nonetheless, the dynamics in your marriage may have contributed to the breakdown of happiness and trust.

And if your goal is to rebuild trust and have a happier marriage moving forward, you must have the humility to examine the part you played in establishing the dynamics in your marriage and home.

Answer the following questions as honestly as you can. Some may be very relevant, others not at all.

• What past complaints has my spouse expressed about me? (i.e. critical, defensive, angry, negative, not supportive, over-spends, not affectionate or sexual, lazy, an indifferent parent, always on the computer or phone, or playing video games etc.)

• What past complaints has my spouse expressed about our marriage or our lifestyle? (i.e. debt load, too busy, disorganized or messy household, skewed priorities, too much technology in the home, opposite-sex friendships, unhealthy diet or lack of exercise, child-centered marriage, no couple time, etc.)

• What complaints have I expressed to my spouse about him/her? Might my spouse be feeling unduly criticized, unloved or unappreciated? How might my complaints have made my spouse feel about himself/herself?

• What complaints have I expressed to my spouse about our marriage or lifestyle? Might my spouse be feeling like I am unhappy with the life we've built together?

• Have I been putting effort into our emotional intimacy? Might my spouse be feeling unimportant, unloved or not prioritized?

- Have I been putting effort into our sexual intimacy? Might my spouse be feeling sexually rejected or unloved?

- Have I been making my spouse feel appreciated?

- Have I been making my spouse feel desired?

- What is the "vibe" in our marriage and home? Does our home have a happy, supportive, easygoing, good-humored vibe? Or does it have a negative, critical and cold vibe?

- Have I been showing love and friendship to my spouse?

- What has been going on in my spouse's life lately? Has my spouse been struggling with any personal or professional issues?

- What has been going on in my life lately? Have I been struggling with any personal or professional issues?

- What appealed to my spouse about the other person? Did my spouse feel needed by the other person? Did he or she feel admired, appreciated or adored by the other person?

- What appealed to my spouse about the situation? Was the situation exciting, liberating, fun or stress-free? Did it bring a "thrill" to the routine of his or her day?

This last question is an important one. Unfaithful spouses are often drawn more toward a situation than a particular person. It is the feelings the situation rouses (i.e. a rush of sexual excitement, freedom or fantasy) that appeals to the spouse.

This realization can help you, the betrayed spouse, "de-personalize" the infidelity or indiscretion and feel less competitive with the other person. It may be that your partner was in love/lust with the feelings, **not** with the other person.

Questions To Ask Your Spouse

There comes a time when spouses who are struggling with broken trust will be ready to have a sincere "heart-to-heart" conversation about why it happened.

This conversation isn't about blaming or hurting each other. It's about understanding why the marriage fell victim to an affair, indiscretion or inappropriate friendship, so that it can be stronger and happier moving forward.

The best heart-to-heart conversations happen naturally and fluidly. Some couples are able to have a conversation that flows freely yet purposefully. They don't need a map to get where they need to go. Other couples need a little direction. It may be that they struggle with expressing themselves verbally or that they have no idea how to even start talking about the infidelity.

Generally, I'm not a fan of "scripted" relationship questions. Too often they come across as forced, artificial and insincere, and that can undermine the authenticity and natural flow of a true heart-to-heart conversation.

That being said, scripted questions can provide a map that can take spouses where they need to go, especially if those spouses don't know how to begin the conversation or don't communicate well verbally. After all, it's certainly better to move forward with a map than to stay in one place spinning your wheels.

The following are a number of questions that you may want to ask your spouse to help you better understand why the trust in your marriage was broken. **Their purpose is to open and facilitate a dialogue. Use them as "talking points."**

Don't worry about sticking to the map. If you ask a question and the answer takes the conversation elsewhere, go with it. The sooner you and your spouse can find your own way to talk about your problems and your marriage, the better.

Read through these questions to see whether they can help. Some may be very relevant to you, others not at all. Although I have included many questions here, I wouldn't recommend tackling too many at once. Be selective and take it slow and steady.

- In what ways were you unhappy with me before the infidelity/indiscretion began?

- In what ways were you unhappy with our marriage, family life or lifestyle before the infidelity/indiscretion began?

- Did you / do you feel appreciated in our marriage?

- Did you / do you feel heard and understood in our marriage?

- Did you/ do you feel like you are a priority to me?

- Did you / do you feel supported in our marriage?

- Do you think we have a child-centered marriage?

- How did you feel about being a parent? What did you/ do you find challenging about it? Do you feel we co-parent well?

- Do you think we've had good emotional intimacy in our marriage? If not, what did you feel was missing?

- Do you think we've had good sexual intimacy in our marriage? If not, what did you feel was missing?

- What do you worry about? (i.e. finances and debt, getting older, health issues, the kids, your aging parents, etc.)

- Was there anything going on in your life, personally or at work, that made you more susceptible to this person or situation?

- Was there anything going on in my life that made you more susceptible to this person or situation?

- How did the other person make you feel?

- How did the situation make you feel? In what ways did it make you feel good? In what ways did it make you feel bad?

- What role do you think technology (i.e. smartphones, texting, computers, social media, etc.) has played in all of this?

- Were you / are you struggling with any stressors or anxiety? If so, were you and I working together to relieve them?

- Before the infidelity/indiscretion, how did you see and feel about yourself? That is, what was your self-perception?

- During the infidelity/indiscretion, how did you see and feel about yourself? That is, what was your self-perception?

- What kind of role models did you have for marriage and how do you think those affected our marriage? What kind of role model do you want to be for our children?

- If we had a time machine and could go back a few years/months, what would you do differently?

- How do you think I contributed to the current state of our marriage? How have I hurt you or let you down?

- How do you think you contributed to the current state of our marriage? How have you hurt me or let me down?

- Do you feel that you and I go through life as allies?

- What do you think might still be standing in the way of our rebuilding trust?

- What do you think might still be standing in the way of our efforts to make our marriage stronger and happier?

- How can we work together to build a fortress around our marriage and family?

Approach these questions with empathy and, as importantly, with a curious spirit. The point is not to debate, disagree with or punish your spouse. The point is to understand why the infidelity or indiscretion happened.

That kind of understanding is important. Once you know where the weakness in your relationship was or is, you can do what's necessary to repair and strengthen it.

Many of the questions presented here necessarily focus on the feelings and needs of the more unfaithful spouse – after all, he or she is the one who broke trust, and you want to find out why.

Yet your needs and feelings are equally important. Most betrayed spouses are desperate for their partner to understand how his or her attitude and behavior contributed to any pre-existing problems in the marriage. They may say, *"You cheated, but I wasn't happy either! You weren't the perfect partner either!"*

In addition, many betrayed spouses want to make their partner understand how his or her infidelity or indiscretion impacted the marriage and/or the family unit. *"Do you have any idea what you put me through?"*

At this point, I just want to reassure you that that discussion will happen. Remember that Part II of this book contains corresponding content. It includes a great deal of insight, instructions and interrelating material and questions for your partner's consideration.

As much as I want you to understand your partner's point of view, I want your partner to understand why he or she did it, how he or she contributed to any pre-existing problems in your relationship, and what impact it had on you and any children.

Try to remember that your partner is doing his or her "part" as well. This is truly a team effort.

Alternatives To "Talking About It"

I'm often asked by spouses whether it's okay to write their partner a letter instead of "talking about it."

My answer is yes, providing that the letter is meant to complement communication and understanding, not just act as substitute for more intimate face-to-face forms of communication.

Letter writing can be useful when a person is dealing with a spouse who is particularly emotional or defensive, and who isn't otherwise receptive to hearing his or her partner out.

Take the case of a wife who is concerned about the deepening friendship her husband is having with a female friend. Every time she broaches the subject, her husband cuts her off and says, "I'm not going to listen to this bullshit. We're just friends!"

When the wife tries to press the matter, the situation soon descends into a fight, the same fight they've had a hundred times over this same issue.

In a situation like this, writing a letter is better than just falling into the same predictable pattern of conflict, defensiveness and anger.

Letter writing can also be helpful for spouses who find it challenging to express themselves verbally, and who need extra time to think through their thoughts and statements.

Some people are very good at putting their foot in their mouth. Writing a letter can help them organize their ideas and write them down in a respectful, coherent way.

For people who are reluctant or embarrassed to share their feelings, letter writing can help them explore and express their emotions without feeling like they're in the spotlight or that they might reveal something they aren't ready to share.

If you choose to write your spouse a letter, be sure to self-check your writing for tone, negativity, accusation, blame and assumption. People always read between the lines, so take care.

Remember that the goal of the letter is to express yourself with honesty and respect, and to encourage your spouse to do likewise. The goal is to open or enhance a dialogue.

The goal of the letter is not to write down every nasty thought you have about your spouse simply because he or she is not there to stop you.

A quick word here about texting. I strongly advise against using text messaging as a way to talk about anything substantial, never mind something as emotional and potentially explosive as infidelity.

Text messages are inherently open to misinterpretation. And whenever a person who reads a text message misinterprets it, he or she always does so in the worst way possible.

A word that is mistakenly sent in ALL CAPS comes across as a loud, angry yell. A message that ends without a heart emoticon comes across as abrupt and insensitive. It just isn't worth the risk.

An alternative to letter-writing, one that people don't think of as much, is voice-recording a message that you can send to your spouse or that spouses can exchange with each other.

Voice recordings can be done on almost any smartphone and have all the advantages of letter writing. They let a spouse speak in a relaxed tone, without being interrupted by the other spouse or facing the other spouse's defensiveness.

Yet they also have an advantage over letter writing because they are able to convey emotion in a more sincere and accurate way. The speaker's tone of voice can limit the guesswork or assumption that sometimes happens when someone reads a written letter.

A voice recording can also act as a take-anywhere message of reassurance from the other spouse.

Whenever a spouse is feeling fearful about the relationship or having flashbacks of anger or suspicion, he or she can simply hit playback on a smartphone and hear his or her spouse's reassuring voice speak words of love, devotion and so on.

So as you can see, there are viable alternatives to "talking about it," or at least to talking it to death. There have to be. People are all different and couples have their own strengths and weaknesses. You have to work with what you have.

Yet many couples who are trying to rebuild trust mistakenly assume that their only choice for professional help is counselling or talk therapy.

Due to the prevalence of talk therapy in our culture, there is certainly the assertion that "talking about it" is the only way to get over it. The more you talk about it, the better.

This idea persists even though talk therapy has a poor success rate in terms of helping couples rebuild their marriages.

It persists even though men in particular are often exceedingly uncomfortable with it. It persists even though many couples say they fight in the car on the drive home from the talk-therapist or counselor's office.

Indeed, a good portion of my clientele has always been comprised of "counselling drop-outs." These are folks who have grown frustrated with the slow, ongoing nature of counselling and of "talking it to death" every week, always digging up the proverbial dead cat and then burying it again.

They're sick of wallowing in the mistake and in the negative emotions and memories that surround it. They're sick of reliving it, pointing fingers and complaining about each other.

Let me be clear: I completely agree that spouses must talk about their problems, feelings, fears, hopes and so on. There is no doubt that talking about the infidelity or indiscretion is necessary for spouses to feel heard and understood, and to agree on changes that must be made if the marriage is to survive and thrive.

But talking is not the only form of communicating a thought or emotion. Sometimes there are more authentic and appropriate ways, especially when our throats are hoarse from talking.

Sometimes a loving embrace can say *"I adore you, I cherish you"* far more intimately than words could.

Sometimes a gentle squeeze of hand or a soft kiss on the cheek can say *"I am sorry"* in a much more sincere way that words could.

Sometimes a warm smile can say *"I know what you're thinking, but I love you and everything will be okay"* in a more heartfelt and reassuring way than words could.

Actions Speak Louder Than Words

Many betrayed spouses know all too well that talk is cheap. They may have asked their spouse "Are you cheating on me?" a hundred times, and a hundred times heard him or her say, "No, I would never cheat on you!" Words don't always speak the truth.

In the end, actions may be more reliable. In fact, I have a little saying that I often tell my clients: If the words and the actions don't match, believe the actions.

For example, let's say a couple is trying to recover after the wife's emotional affair. The husband asks her, "Did you text him today?"

She says, "No," but then refuses to let her husband look at her phone which, incidentally, is password protected. This doesn't exactly convey a sense of trustworthiness, does it?

Now let's say the wife leaves her cell phone – unlocked and fully accessible to her husband – on the kitchen counter at all times.

Whenever he wants, he can pick it up and scroll through the messages. In this case, the husband may not even ask if she has texted the other man. Her actions make the question unnecessary.

Spouses, even those in conflict, usually know each other pretty well. They know what makes each other happy, sad, reassured, fearful.

They know what actions they can take to make each other's days easier and nights more enjoyable.

If they are motivated, they can recall their spouse's complaints and, by putting some thought into it, come up with ways to address those complaints for the greater good of the marriage.

Consider this example. A husband has been complaining that he doesn't feel appreciated by his wife. She says, "Well, tell me what I can do to make you feel appreciated?"

He answers, "I don't know...maybe get the kids to take better care of their electronics so that I don't feel like I'm working for nothing."

The next day, the kids are fooling around when they break a costly video-game controller. The wife chastises the kids and says, "Your dad wants you to take better care of your things!"

The husband storms out of the room. The wife follows him and says, "Why are you pissed off? I did what you said!"

The husband throws up his arms. "You didn't do anything! You just managed to make me look like the bad guy yet again."

How different would this have played out if, once the wife knew the husband's complaint – feeling unappreciated by her and their children – she put some thought into more sincere ways to make him feel appreciated.

For example, she might have met her husband at the door after work and encouraged her children to do the same saying, "Let's welcome dad home. He's worked hard all day."

I'm willing to bet that this simple act of thoughtfulness and appreciation would mean more to this husband than a video-game controller.

These are simple examples, but they illustrate an important point. **Spouses who are trying to rebuild trust need to focus on their actions. Our actions can convey our thoughts, feelings and priorities in some very powerful ways.**

Although it is your spouse who has broken the trust in your relationship, there are nonetheless many things you can do to help improve the overall dynamics in the marriage.

After all, the happier your spouse is with you, the more likely it is that he or she will remain motivated to restoring trust and to changing for the better.

Ask yourself: When were we the happiest as a couple? When did my spouse seem to be the most in love with me?

These questions are a fantastic starting point. It may be that you and your spouse were the happiest when you used to surprise each other with week-end getaways. Try to do that again.

Even if your circumstances have changed – let's say you have kids or don't have as much disposable income – you can still reproduce the freedom of the experience to some extent, even if it's just by leaving the kids at grandma's for the night and having a dinner-and-movie night at home.

It may be that, once you start thinking about it, you realize your spouse seemed most in love with you when you encouraged him or her spend time with friends or engage in a favorite hobby.

You may remember that your spouse seemed happiest and treated you the best when you had more outside interests and the two of you weren't spending every minute together.

You may begin to compare the way you speak to and interact with your spouse now with the way you used to speak to and interact with your spouse, and in the process you may realize that your voice tone has become critical and your behavior has become cold and indifferent.

And as you do this, your spouse notices the change. He or she notices your efforts to spend child-free nights together, to give him or her more social time with good friends, and to take responsibility for your own happiness by re-embracing your own interests.

Your spouse notices the softer tones in your voice and the way you reach out to give him or her a gentle caress on the shoulder or a kiss on the cheek.

And as your spouse delights in these efforts and changes, he or she is motivated to make similar efforts and changes for you. Loving behavior sparks loving behavior. Kind words spark kind words. Effort and change spark effort and change.

Emotional & Sexual Intimacy

Happy couples know an important truth about marriage: emotional and sexual intimacy are two sides of the same coin. This coin must always remain spinning so that the value of both sides can be seen.

If one side is always up while the other is turned down, or if one side is assumed to have more value than the other side, problems are going to happen. There's no way around it.

This is often seen as the classic "love vs. sex" debate; however, emotional intimacy isn't just about feeling loved. It's also about feeling appreciated, adored, respected, desired and validated. It's about being recognized for who you are.

Emotional intimacy is enhanced by talking, touching, laughing, supporting and prioritizing each other. It is strengthened by working "as a team" in all things, including resolving conflict.

Sexual intimacy – believe it or not – is about many of the same things. Why? Because a person who does not feel loved, appreciated, desired and so on by their spouse is unlikely to feel the full spectrum of pleasure that true sexual intimacy provides.

Of course, spouses may gravitate toward one side or the other. A husband may feel more loving toward his wife, and be willing to show her more non-sexual affection, when she is having frequent and enjoyable sex with him.

At the same time, his wife may feel more sexually attracted to him, and be willing to engage in more frequent and enjoyable sex, when he is showing her more non-sexual affection.

You can see how that creates a vicious circle, right? It also creates a "you go first" mentality where spouses basically wait each other out in what can best be described as a pissing contest:

> *"I'm not going to have sex with you until I feel more loved and supported outside the bedroom."*

> vs.

> *"Why should I help you if you won't even have sex with me? My needs are important too, you know."*

It's a deadlock. But it's a deadlock that's easy enough to break if one partner chooses to prioritize his or her spouse's needs, thereby sending the message that re-establishing intimacy is more important than getting the other person to "give in."

A caveat here: I'm not suggesting that a spouse have sex with a partner who isn't acting in a loving or respectful way. Doing so will only create more problems. I am, however, suggesting that showing your spouse that you care about his or her needs can motivate that partner to care about your needs.

Many spouses who are struggling with some form of infidelity or indiscretion will say they didn't feel their emotional and/or sexual needs for intimacy were being met in the marriage.

Meeting these needs isn't just necessary to rebuild trust and save a marriage. It is also necessary to prevent breaches of trust from happening again.

"When Should We Sleep Together Again?"

While there's no "right" answer to this question, here is my general guideline: When both spouses understand that emotional and sexual intimacy are two sides of the same coin, and when both spouses are committed to meeting each other's needs for them, then it's probably okay to start sleeping together again.

Don't get me wrong – other factors may need to be present as well, such as a clean bill of sexual health, an assurance that the extramarital relationship has ended, a genuine display of remorse or a few productive heart-to-heart conversations.

Ultimately, it should be up to the spouse whose trust was broken to decide whether he or she is ready to have sex with his or her spouse again. A betrayed spouse should never feel pressured.

Two Steps Forward, One Step Back:
How To Signal Your Spouse For Support

Earlier in this part of the book I touched on triggers. These are the emotions – fear, sadness, insecurity, and many others – that can cause a person to lash out in any number of ways. Memories and thought processes can trigger emotional outbursts, too.

As a betrayed spouse, there will be times when you find that your memories, thoughts and emotions turn toward some very unpleasant things.

This can happen even if much time has passed, and even if you and your partner have made real progress in terms of rebuilding trust and strengthening your marriage.

It is perfectly normal for a spouse whose trust has been broken to experience mental and emotional flashbacks, even very intense ones; however, it can be very disheartening for a couple, especially if they have begun to think that the worst is behind them.

A betrayed spouse may say, "I'll never get over this," while the unfaithful spouse may say, "I thought you were over this?" When this happens, many couples begin to argue and talk about the infidelity or indiscretion as if it had just happened.

To avoid falling into this "talking it to death" trap, I often recommend that the spouse whose trust has been broken recognize his or her triggers and have a "signal" that he or she can send the other spouse when bad memories, feelings or flashbacks strike.

For example, take the case of a stay-at-home mom and wife whose husband had a sexual affair a year ago.

They have worked hard to rebuild trust and improve their marriage; however, every now and then, the wife's mind begins to wander.

This tends to happen after she has put her baby daughter down for her morning nap. The house is quiet and she has time to sit at the kitchen table alone and think...and to think back.

And that's exactly what she does. She thinks back to every gory detail, every lie and deception, every secret rendezvous, every hurt and heartache.

By the time her husband gets home after work, she is in angry tears and the fight is on. Again.

In this case, the wife tends to be triggered by silence and idleness. If she were more aware of that, she would be able to take steps to avoid being triggered (or at least to avoid being triggered as often).

She might choose to play music or call a friend during that time. She might choose to exercise or to work on a project.

In addition, she could "signal" her spouse for support by sending a short text message that lets him know she needs some kind of reassurance from him.

This signal might be something that they have agreed upon together, such as the year they were married.

When the husband receives a text from her that reads "2012," he knows that he needs to give her a quick call or reassuring text to show his support.

These signals can happen in person, too. Let's say a couple is enjoying a social event when the husband sees a man who looks disconcertingly like the man his wife had an affair with.

Instead of letting his thoughts and emotions get away from him like a runaway train, he signals his wife – perhaps by rubbing his hands together – that he needs her support.

When she sees this, she makes an extra effort to be affectionate and loving to him.

When it comes to rebuilding trust after an affair or indiscretion, long-term thinking is essential. You must be in it for the long haul. You must know that it will sometimes seem like you're taking two steps forward and one step back.

Yet by:

a) knowing your triggers
b) taking steps to manage them, and
c) sending out signals for support to your partner

...you can ensure that the steps forward get bigger every day.

"When Should I Give Up Or Stop Trying?"

To be sure, there are cases where a marriage has been so awful that it is in the best interests of the spouse (and his or her children) to end the marriage.

The same can be said of attempts to rebuild trust or reconcile when those do more harm than good.

Cases that involve any kind of abuse or intimidation, high-conflict personalities, untreated mental illness or addiction stand apart.

In such instances, the priority isn't restoring trust or saving the marriage – it's staying safe, getting out and getting help.

Some experts believe that infidelity is a form of emotional abuse. It's certainly a time of emotional turmoil that affects every aspect of our lives, from our physical health and self-perception to our career performance and the way we parent our children.

As much as I believe that infidelity can be overcome and that marriages can go on to be happier and stronger than ever, I know that sometimes, unfortunately, that can't happen.

When it comes to the question, "When should I stop trying?" you must do some soul-searching and follow your gut.

One person cannot form an alliance. That's the whole point of this book's two-part structure and collaborative content.

One spouse cannot put in the work while the other simply points fingers, gets defensive, refuses to make consistent changes, or storms off in a fit of belligerence or indifference.

Are you seeing true effort on your spouse's part? Has that effort been consistent and progressive?

That is, is your spouse's behavior getting better over time? Are you doing your part?

Still, I know you're looking for something more concrete. Earlier in this part of the book, I talked about the value of putting a timeline on a spouse's indecision to stay or go. I think that's a workable approach here, too.

But how long should that timeline be?

Again, a "seasonal" approach often works well. A betrayed spouse might say, "I'll give this an honest try until the New Year," or "until the kids are out of school in the summer."

There comes a point where trying to rebuild trust – especially if an unfaithful spouse isn't motivated or cannot be relied upon to make consistent changes – becomes more about delaying divorce than avoiding it.

This isn't the voice of doom talking here. It's just something to keep in the back of your mind.

How To Prevent It From Happening Again

Many couples successfully rebuild their marriages after trust has been broken. Some even say they are better off because of it. The affair, indiscretion or inappropriate opposite-sex friendship forced them to face the weak spots in their marriage. It forced them to work together to repair and strengthen them.

For some couples, this crisis marked the first time they worked together as allies to do anything positive. I sincerely hope that will be your experience, and that this book can help you make it happen.

I encourage you to flip through the pages of this book from time to time, and especially during those times you feel a strain on your marriage. Doing so can remind you of some simple yet powerful strategies that can keep your marital alliance strong.

I will leave you with ten snapshot strategies that encompass some of the big-picture ideas put forth in this book. These are concepts that can affair-proof and divorce-proof a marriage.

By incorporating these strategies into your relationship on a daily basis, you will be laying the foundation for a marriage and home that is built on very strong ground indeed.

1. **Listen to your spouse's complaints or concerns.** It is foolish, short-sighted and selfish to shrug off a partner's complaints, whether they are about housework, money, a lack of affection, in-laws or texting.

   It is even worse to become ignorant or defensive when your partner tries to express the reasons for his or her unhappiness. You don't need to agree; however, you do need to listen, care and do something to improve the situation.

   Keep your ears open: when you hear your partner express something he or she is unhappy with in the marriage or home, stop what you're doing and listen. Instead of just arguing, show your spouse that you care about his or her happiness and are willing to work together.

2. **Express your own complaints or concerns.**   Instead of bottling up your feelings and expecting your spouse to read your mind, be open about whatever it is that is bothering you. Just be sure that you always do this in a way that is productive and respectful of your partner's feelings and perspective.

   If the issue is an emotional or potentially volatile one, set the conversation up for success by choosing a good time to talk and by setting a positive mood.

3. **Build a fortress around your marriage.** Strong marriages have a wall of privacy around them. This wall keeps in feelings of love, devotion, respect, friendship and family solidarity. It shields the marriage from the view of outsiders while allowing for total transparency inside, between spouses (i.e. shared passwords on phones and computers).

   This wall also keeps certain things out, including destructive emotions or assumptions, negative behaviors, and people would could potentially chip away at a couple's bond (i.e. opposite-sex friends and intruding in-laws).

4. **Put technology in its place.** Translation: Put down the damn phone and talk to your spouse and kids! Log out of social media and have a movie night with your family. Stop texting friends or pointlessly surfing the Internet and start connecting with the people that matter in your life. Fight the impulse to check your phone for messages or email every five minutes. Put your phone in a drawer at night and engage in some pillow-talk with your sweetheart instead.

5. **Speak to and interact with your spouse like he or she is someone you love.** Speak with love – not criticism, contempt or defensiveness – in your voice tone. Use positive body language. Remember your manners. Greet your spouse at the door with a kiss. Praise your spouse in front of your children.

Offer a smile instead of a frown, a flirtatious wink instead of a scowl. Caress your partner's shoulder as you walk by him or her. Be someone that your spouse wants to come home to. There are a hundred ways you can show your spouse, every day, that you are grateful to have him or her in your life.

6. **Nourish emotional intimacy.** Stay tuned-in to what is happening in your spouse's life. Is he or she going through a hard time at work? Is he or she trying to eat healthier? Whatever it is, use it as an opportunity to show your spouse that a) you actually notice what is going on in his or her life and b) you truly care and are there to offer encouragement and support.

   Remind yourself often that your spouse isn't just a fixture in your home – he or she is a human being with his or her own feelings, fears, hopes and struggles. Shower your spouse with respect, appreciation, adoration, non-sexual affection, true friendship and love.

7. **Don't let sex fall off the radar.** Sex is a big part of marriage. In fact, regular sexual access to a person they love is a prevailing reason that people get married. Order-in supper more often, put the kids to bed earlier, chew on a handful of chocolate-covered coffee beans before bed — do whatever it takes to keep some energy for sex.

As importantly, be sure that your sex life remains fun and pleasurable. Let your spouse know that you desire him or her by showing sexual enthusiasm and taking the initiative to "spice it up" once in a while with sex toys, erotica, etc.

8. **Put your spouse's needs and happiness ahead of your own.** This doesn't mean that your needs or happiness come second. The needs and happiness of both spouses in a marriage are equal; however, by putting your spouse ahead of yourself, you set the tone for a marriage where both spouses are "competing" to meet each other's needs and make each other happy. Now *that's* a dream marriage.

9. **Create a happy household vibe.** Most of us have walked into a house where you feel like you could cut the tension with a knife. Those who live there are growly, argumentative and seem to actively dislike one another. Most of us have walked into a different type of house too, the type where warmth and happiness envelopes you as soon as you pass through the door. Those who live there seem to genuinely enjoy each other's company. The vibe is easygoing, friendly and relaxed.

   Strive for the latter household! Create a happy vibe in your home where your spouse and your children co-exist in love, friendship and good-humor. Work as allies with your spouse and/or kids to share household duties and domestic chores, always showing your appreciation for their solidarity and support.

10. Be a whole person. It's a fact of married life: happy spouses make happy marriages. A person who is at peace with his or her life and who strives to exhibit positive personality traits (i.e. open-mindedness, an easygoing nature, good humor, emotional control, reliability, humility, etc.) is far more likely to be a loving and loved spouse than someone who doesn't have these qualities.

Strive to be the best, happiest person you can be outside of your marriage and you will find that your marriage reflects who you are.

Part II

To Be Read By The Spouse Who Broke Trust

Where To Go From Here?

If your genuine goal is to keep your marriage and/or family together, you're reading the right book. I will tell you what you need to hear, even if it isn't want you want to hear. It may be the hardline at times. You can take it. And I applaud you for that.

Let's start with your options. Assuming your goal is to keep your marriage together, it looks to me like you have two of them:

1. Make a half-hearted attempt to earn back your spouse's trust and love. Begrudgingly agree to talk or be transparent, always keeping that edge of resentment in your voice. When your spouse becomes emotional or asks for something, exhale heavily with a sigh of irritation. When your spouse expresses her or his feelings, rise up in defensiveness or impatience or – better yet – blame.

2. Make a sincere attempt to earn back your spouse's trust and love. Strive to understand how deeply your actions have wounded the person you promised to cherish more than anyone else in the world. Put humility in your heart and prioritize your spouse's needs, patiently doing what is necessary to restore trust, love, devotion and friendship to your marriage. When the time is right, respectfully and lovingly express your own complaints and needs so that the marriage, moving forward, can be happier for both of you.

It's your call.

Why You Need To Put Your Spouse First

Let's face it. Many people who have been engaging in an extramarital affair, opposite-sex friendship or various indiscretions have been living by the "it's all about me" motto for a while. They've been focused on their own pleasure and fulfillment.

In some cases, an unfaithful spouse has even been viewing his or her spouse as a type of "enemy" for some time. After all, a suspicious spouse can be annoying: they're always asking where you're going, who you're texting and what's going on. They make it hard at times to connect with a more exciting and fresh-faced person – the extramarital lover or "friend."

That kind of self-focus has to change, right now. For the time-being, the focus has to be on your spouse. But what about your complaints or needs, you ask? That's a fair question.

Picture this: a couple arrives by ambulance in the emergency department after being in a car accident. One spouse has a broken arm and various bruises, and is in a lot of pain.

The other spouse has several broken ribs, massive internal injuries and is in a severe state of shock. His or her blood pressure is dropping and he or she is dying on the table.

Which spouse do you think should be treated first?

It may be that you have complaints in the marriage. It may be that your spouse hasn't been a perfect partner either. In my experience, negative or dysfunctional dynamics in the marriage often to contribute to infidelity; however, there is a time and place for an unfaithful spouse to express his or her complaints and needs. We're not there yet. We'll get there soon, though.

For the moment, it's all about your spouse.

Apologizing vs. Acknowledging

One of the biggest mistakes an unfaithful spouse makes after his or her infidelity or indiscretion has been discovered is to overuse the phrase, "I'm sorry!"

It's even worse if the message is, "I already said I'm sorry, what else do you want me to say?!"

To many betrayed spouses, the phrase "I'm sorry" actually sounds like: "I got busted, I said I'm sorry, now drop it." Even an unfaithful spouse who is sincerely apologetic and filled with regret and guilt can unintentionally send this message by over-apologizing.

Why? Because an apology is self-focused. It's about excusing your behavior. An acknowledgement is different – it focuses on the impact your behavior had on the other person.

That is a critical distinction to make. In fact, I recommend re-reading the above paragraph. This distinction is so critical that I'm going to drive home the point with an example.

Let's say you own a rare antique convertible car. You've spent years and a small fortune restoring it, searching for parts and accessories that are hard to find, and now it's in mint condition. You love it and sometimes find yourself gazing at its gleaming paint on the driveway. You take your friends and family for summer drives to the ice-cream shop in it, making wonderful memories.

Then one day, your neighbor backs into it.

Scenario 1: Your neighbor says, "I'm sorry," and hands you his insurance info. Then he goes inside his house and has supper.

Scenario 2: Your neighbor says, "I am so sorry," and stays with you on the street, scrutinizing every inch of the car for damage. He says, "I know how much work and money you've put into this car, and how much it means to you. It's more than just a set of wheels, it's your baby. I feel terrible and I know how hard it will be to find replacement parts. I'll help you look. I'll pay for the damage, but I'll also help you put it back together until it's perfect."

The first scenario is an apology. The second scenario is an acknowledgement. What comes across as more authentic? What scenario moves you toward forgiveness faster?

What scenario makes it more likely that you will continue to have a good relationship with your neighbor?

One of the biggest complaints I hear from betrayed spouses is that their spouse just "doesn't get it." That is, the unfaithful spouse doesn't fully acknowledge or understand the emotional impact his or her actions have had on the other spouse.

A betrayed spouse needs to know that his or her partner understands and acknowledges the depth of pain, anger, betrayal, heartbreak, shock and hurt that he or she has caused.

If your spouse doesn't think that you "get it," he or she will never trust you again. It's too big of a risk. Consider the car example. Which neighbor do you trust to be more careful backing out of his driveway alongside your precious convertible?

Of course, the neighbor who acknowledged how his actions impacted you is more believable. He's more trustworthy. He's the type of guy that you know will now be extra-careful backing out of his driveway. He's a low-risk to hit your car again.

In addition to acknowledging the emotional and mental impact your behavior has had on your spouse (and perhaps on your family unit), an unfaithful spouse needs to acknowledge that the infidelity or indiscretion was entirely his or her own fault.

As I've said, you may have legitimate complaints about your marriage and your spouse's behavior. It may be that the unhappy dynamics in the marriage did contribute to the infidelity.

Again, that's something that will be addressed later. My goal isn't to persuade you to stay in an unhappy marriage. **My goal is to help you rebuild trust so that the larger work of making the marriage a happier and stronger one for both of you can happen.**

But here's the truth of it: you are the one who broke trust. Regardless of what was happening in the marriage, that didn't have to happen. The sooner you take full responsibility for that, the better. This is not the time to defend or excuse your actions, or to blame your spouse for your actions.

Have you ever had a job you didn't like? Maybe you didn't get along with your boss or you didn't get paid enough. Did that give you the right to steal from the company? Of course not.

You could have tried to improve the relationship with your boss or ask for a raise, perhaps by being a better employee. And if that didn't work, you could have resigned. There was no need to resort to stealing. You had other options, but you didn't take them.

You get it, right?

Acknowledgement is double-sided. One side involves proving to your spouse that you understand how your behavior impacted her or him. It involves owning up to the seriousness of what you've done, rather than trying to downplay it. The other side involves taking full responsibility for your behavior.

Attitude Adjustments

It isn't just the betrayed spouse that gets hit with a wave of emotion following the discovery of an extramarital affair or inappropriate friendship. As the spouse who has broken trust, you will also experience a range of feelings.

You may feel embarrassed or attacked, controlled or condemned. You may feel sad, guilty, regretful or angry. You may feel belittled or resentful, shameful or scared. The list goes on.

 Emotions are strange things. We sometimes feel one but express another. A husband who feels embarrassed or guilty over his infidelity may lash out in ugly belligerence to the wife he has betrayed, as if trying to ignore or deny the reality of what he has done. He may even try to blame her for his behavior.

A wife who feels shame or sadness over her infidelity may lash out to the husband she has betrayed, demanding that he decide, right now, whether or not he is willing to forgive her.

In both cases, the unfaithful spouse comes across as having – to put it very plainly – a bad attitude.

Monitor yourself for this kind of "bad attitude" behavior. In the aftermath of an infidelity, your spouse needs you at your very best. He or she needs to know that you are an ally, not an enemy. So act like an ally at all times.

If you've broken your spouse's trust, you may have a long road ahead of you before you can rebuild that trust. **To start the journey off right, burn these three qualities into your soul:**

1. **Empathy**. This is the ability to feel what your spouse is feeling. When you see your spouse crying, raging, trembling, falling apart, looking fearful or heartbroken, or withdrawing into silence and solitude – well, do something about it. Be there, even if it is just to hold him or her. Let him or her know that you understand.

2. **Humility**. This is the ability to recognize that it isn't all about you. It is the ability to see and be accountable for your own shortcomings, to have a realistic and modest view of your own importance, and to realize that your partner isn't to blame for your actions or for all your marriage problems (some perhaps, but not all).

3. **Patience.** This is the ability to show self-restraint, maturity and understanding to your spouse even during those times you feel irritated or fed-up with his or her emotions or questions. It is the ability to help your spouse through this crisis without becoming angry or intolerant when he or she doesn't "get over it" as quickly as you might like. In fact, the words "get over it" should never pass your lips.

To be honest, I've never seen a couple move past infidelity in a complete or consistent way where the unfaithful spouse didn't master these abilities. They are absolutely necessary. As healing starts to happen, they are qualities that you too must master to rebuild your marriage alliance.

Were You Tempted By Technology?

A few decades ago, infidelity was comparably straightforward: there were sexual affairs, one-night-stands and emotional affairs. It could be tricky to start an affair, too.

First of all, you'd have to "make the moves" in person, risking whether or not the object of your desire would be game to play along.

You might find yourself having to call the person's home – remember, there are no cell phones – and risk an angry spouse answering the phone with, "Who the hell is this? And why do you want to talk to my wife/husband?" This could make it a challenge to arrange meet-ups.

All of that changed with the rise of personal technology (smartphones, tablets, computers) and social media. Now, it is relatively easy and risk-free to toy with infidelity.

All you have to do is send a winking emoticon or innocent "hi how r u?" text to someone and see whether he or she takes the bait. Or even better, you might receive that text and think, "Hey, this is kind of exciting. It can't hurt to play along for a while."

Text messages that begin as "innocent" exchanges between opposite-sex friends or acquaintances are notorious for escalating, at the speed of light, to intimate and sexually explicit chats and pics. Countless infidelities and indiscretions start this way.

The medium of text provides a false sense of intimacy and friendship that people, especially those who might be a little bored or unhappy in their marriage, quickly over-value.

They become preoccupied with the illusion of the relationship and the sexual thrill of it all. Before you know it, they're racing for their smartphone every time it beeps, hoping for the thrill of a text message from their "friend."

Such pseudo-relationships are easy to carry on, too. Just change the password on your smartphone or computer and remember to delete the conversations, and you're good.

In fact, you can even carry on an inappropriate conversation with another person at your own kitchen table, with your spouse and children only an arm's length away.

If your spouse asks who you're texting, that's easy – just accuse her or him of being paranoid or controlling, and tell her or him that it's private.

Social media sites are similarly tempting and facilitate infidelity. It's all too easy for a spouse to contact or be contacted by a past partner and to find that a few initial innocent exchanges have ramped up into intimate conversation and picture exchanges.

Again, this medium fools people into believing that they have connected on a deep, meaningful level with this other person; however, the relationship is nothing more than an illusion.

After all, you never see this person at their worst – first thing in the morning, yelling at their kids, feeling sick or grumpy – you just assume they are always as fresh, exciting and positive as they come across on the screen.

But what if you want to have that sense of sexual excitement without connecting with a "real" person in your life? Well, the Internet has that solved, too. There are countless dating, hook-up and "friend finder" websites and apps that facilitate anonymous sexual connections and conversations.

In only a matter of minutes, a person can create a fake online profile and engage in the type of sexually explicit dialogue that would make a sailor blush.

Whether these exchanges remain anonymous and voyeuristic or whether they progress into in-person meetings is anyone's call. Either way, it stays private.

Or does it? Here's the thing about technology – nothing is ever private. One way or another, many people who engage in this kind of behavior get caught.

They forget to lock their smartphone. They forget to log-out of a site. They leave some kind of trail that their spouse is eventually going to discover, whether by complete accident or because they were suspicious and went digging for it.

Ask yourself: What role, if any, did personal forms of technology and social media play in all of this? How did they contribute to the breach of trust in your marriage?

Coming Clean: What You Should Reveal

It could be that you've been having a long-term sexual affair. It could be that you had a one-time sexual indiscretion. It could be that you've been visiting escorts, paying for sex or communicating on various sex-chat websites or online dating sites.

It could be that you've been carrying on an inappropriate opposite-sex friendship via text messages, social media or in person, one that has become – or is becoming – an emotional affair. It could be almost anything.

No doubt your spouse is full of questions. Some betrayed spouses will lash out at their partner with a barrage of questions, accusations and assumptions. Others may retreat into silence; however you can read the questions on their face.

Some of these questions may be easier for you to answer than others. You may be anxious to spare your spouse's feelings, perhaps fearing the situation will spiral out of control. You may also be anxious to protect your extramarital partner or friend.

Regardless, there are certain answers that your spouse is reasonably entitled to. Before you can move forward, it is likely that you will have to reveal some essential information:

- Who have you been seeing or talking to?
- What form did the breach of trust take?

Was it:

a) Sexual

b) Emotional

c) Tech-based

d) A combination of these

- How did it start and how long has it been going on?
- If you met up in person, where and how often?
- How did you communicate with this other person?
- Are you still communicating with this other person?
- Is the extramarital relationship over or still going on?

A betrayed spouse often feels like the floor has dropped out from below them. Their world is spinning. The uncertainty of their situation makes them feel like they can't find solid footing.

That feeling is intensified and exacerbated when the unfaithful spouse withholds information that can begin to put the pieces together.

It is unrealistic to expect your spouse to work on the marriage without knowing the identity of the other person, the nature of the relationship, how you communicated and whether the extramarital relationship and contact have ended.

You may not want to provide this information. It may cause problems for you in ways that your spouse doesn't understand. But as I said at the beginning of this part, you're either committed to rebuilding your marriage or you aren't.

You need to prove to your spouse that you are serious about restoring trust and saving your marriage. Withholding this kind of information sends precisely the opposite message.

Downplaying the importance of your spouse obtaining these answers – *"What's the point of knowing who it is? It's over so it doesn't matter!"* – sends an insensitive and controlling message to your spouse: Your needs are irrelevant. We'll do it my way.

Getting Your Priorities Straight

Some spouses who have been involved with another person, especially if it's been going on for a while, get their priorities skewed. They may feel a sense of concern or obligation toward the other person. That is misplaced loyalty in the extreme.

I guarantee it, nothing will sink your marriage faster than dividing your loyalties between your spouse and an extramarital partner or friend.

The very notion of that is antithetical to the "above all others" virtue of marriage itself. You know it. Your spouse knows it, too.

It may be that you have feelings for this person or, just as likely, that you enjoy the feelings you have when you are with him or her. It isn't the person per se, it is the situation.

Regardless, if your spouse feels that you are prioritizing the other person's feelings or well-being over his or her own, any attempts to rebuild the marriage will be over before they begin.

Why It's Unfair To Compare

It sometimes happens that a spouse will compare his or her spouse with an extramarital lover or friend, whether consciously or not. Consider the following example.

Karen and Jack had been married for ten years. A year earlier, Jack's company had down-sized and he had been laid off. Since then, he had been a stay-at-home dad while Karen continued to work as a lawyer. It was a good arrangement, as both felt it benefited their children and let them maintain a flexible lifestyle.

Yet as the months went on, Karen found that Jack was less and less interesting to come home to. All he talked about was what the kids did that day, what he had watched on television, or how exhausted he was after chasing after two toddlers all day.

On top of that, he had started to gain some weight and a somewhat irritating streak of insecurity was showing up. He often said, "I feel like I should be making the money...it's kind of embarrassing, to be honest." Karen found herself rolling her eyes.

Soon, Karen struck up a friendship with a co-worker, a lawyer named Frank. Frank was new to the firm and was a breath of fresh air in an otherwise stuffy office.

Plus, he was easy on the eyes. The women in the office couldn't help but look when he walked by. He was fit, dressed impeccably and always had something fascinating or funny to say. He was a classic flirt too, and always had a sweet compliment ready to give any woman, young or old, attractive or plain.

Karen liked the fact that, of all the women in the office, Frank seemed to gravitate toward her. He surprised her with her favorite coffee and started to send her flirtatious text messages.

Before long, the text messages weren't limited to office hours. Karen would be sitting beside Jack on the couch at home, listening to him talk about the kids, when the 'bing' of Frank's texts would come in. As always, they were funny and interesting.

Karen started to leave the room to text Frank back. Their exchanges became increasingly frequent and intimate. Jack – feeling even more insecure – asked Karen who she was texting so often. Karen sighed with irritation and said, "It's nobody, Jack. A co-worker. Stop being paranoid."

As Karen watched Jack – frazzled and familiar – drag their kids off to bed, she couldn't help but think of Frank's warm smile and the way he was starting to flash her a mischievous wink whenever she walked by.

She began to grow more and more irritated by Jack. He was always so predictable and so stressed. His weight gain had made him self-conscious and he was having problems performing in bed.

Karen doubted that Frank ever had that problem.

Ouch, right? Unfortunately, unfaithful or straying spouses often make these kinds of conscious or unconscious comparisons. The example here is of a wife, but if often happens the other way too, where a husband compares his wife – his familiar, frazzled wife – with the fresh-faced, energetic new secretary or gym buddy.

As we all know, it's a cold and cruel world out there. Most of us are constantly sold the message by media and our culture that we are too old, too fat, too poor, too everything.

The last place we need to hear this message is in our marriage and home; however, when a spouse compares his or her spouse to a fresher face, that's exactly what happens. It's cruel to compare your spouse to someone else.

It's also unfair. In many cases, an extramarital partner is single, divorced or has few obligations. He or she has all the time in the world to look handsome or pretty, to work-out, to shop for clothes and to present himself or herself as always attractive, always happy, always caring, always fascinating and fresh-faced.

Most of the time, it's total bullshit. It's a smoke-screen for a wreck of a person who is so insecure or desperate for attention that he or she would knowingly become involved with a married person. This is even more true if the married person has children.

The amazingness of the other person is always an illusion. Their appeal may be due to nothing more than how unfamiliar they are to you, or how little you really know about their true self.

Turn the situation around: What if your spouse – consciously or not – compared your attractiveness, physique, age, abilities or income to a better looking, more fit, younger, more skilled and wealthier person of your gender?

What if that person had every opportunity to present himself or herself as the world's most fascinating and flawless person, while you were saddled with the burden of familiarity and obligations? If that wouldn't bother you, you're a little less human than the rest of us.

But affairs don't just happen between a married person and a single or divorced person. There are many cases that involve partners who are both married to other people.

Again, it can be easy to compare our familiar spouse to someone else's unfamiliar spouse. It's voyeuristic. And if the other person is crying on our shoulder about how unhappy he or she is in the marriage, we may begin to wonder why his or her spouse would treat such an amazing person so poorly?

Hmmm. Perhaps it's because the other person isn't quite as amazing as we think. Illusions always fade upon examination.

Is It Love or Lust?

Nonetheless, affairs and infidelity can be complicated things and it sometimes happens that a person believes he or she is genuinely in love with the extramarital partner or friend.

This is especially so if a person has been unhappy in their marriage. Perhaps they have been treated poorly by their spouse or their spouse hasn't been meeting their needs for emotional or sexual intimacy.

For example, a wife whose husband is constantly critical or belligerent may be very drawn to a man with a kinder, gentler spirit. It is easy for him to make her feel respected and admired.

A husband who is constantly being sexually rejected by his wife may be drawn to a flirtatious co-worker. It is easy for her to make him feel desirable and appreciated.

These examples may come across as stereotypes, but they are extremely common scenarios and they happen all the time.

So what should you do if you don't know whether the attraction you feel for the extramarital partner is love or lust?

For starters, answer the following questions. The more you answer "No," the more likely it is than your affair is driven by hormonal lust and illusion, not genuine love.

• Have you performed mundane duties with this person (i.e. yardwork, shopping, home repairs, financial planning, co-parenting, getting insurance quotes, etc.)?

• Have you spent time with, or money on, this person's parents, siblings, family and close friends?

• If you suddenly became bankrupt, would this person stand by you and do whatever it took to financially recover (i.e. live in a basement suite and take a dishwashing job to support you)?

• Have you seen this person at his or her worst (i.e. sick, emotional, stressed, etc.)?

• Would you be proud to introduce this person to your children, parents, family and friends? Would you be proud to share the details of this person's past, and how your relationship began?

• If this person died or became incapacitated today, would you be willing to raise his or her children as your own and settle his or her outstanding debts? Would you be willing to pay for this person's ongoing medical care? Would you be willing to pay for his or her children's medical, educational and other living costs?

• If you died or became incapacitated today, would you give this person Power of Attorney over your finances, assets, minor children and personal health decisions? Would you trust him or her to manage your children's trust fund or care for your aging parents?

• If you were to leave your underage children in this person's care right now, are you just as confident that he or she would take as many measures to protect your children from harm (i.e. not leaving them in the car unattended, watching them in a crowd) as your current spouse would?

• If you could never have a sexual relationship with this person, would you still put as much effort into seeing her or him?

These questions may sound plodding, but that's the point. Love puts down roots and takes time to grow. Lust is a faster ride. It's a roller coaster that people sometimes hop onto for a thrill.

The sudden loops give you butterflies but, without love to keep you on the rails, the ride always ends abruptly and usually with nothing to show for it but a sickening feeling in the pit of your stomach.

In a new and healthy relationship between two single/available people, lust is the force that draws them together and motivates them to stay together so that their romance has time to mature and transition to genuine feelings of love.

If you do it right, you lust after your partner until you fall in love with him or her. And then you keep the spark alive through the ups and downs of your marriage so that you can enjoy both lust and love for the rest of your lives.

Should You Always Follow Your Feelings?

Here's a dicey question: What if, even after challenging yourself and doing a reality check, you still believe that the feelings you have toward your extramarital partner or friend are true love?

Well, it now becomes a question of choice, not feelings. Will you choose to uphold the promises you've made to your spouse to work through your problems, for better or for worse?

Will you choose to uphold the obligations you have to the children you have deliberately brought into the world with your spouse?

The truth is, none of us have the freedom to follow our feelings whenever we want, however we want and whatever the consequences.

There are mornings we don't feel like going to work. There are times we don't feel like interacting with our children or being patient with them. There are times we don't feel like helping a friend move or talking for hours to a distraught friend.

My intention isn't to trivialize feelings you may have for your extramarital partner or persuade you to "pick" your spouse. My intention is to give you another way to think about this situation. Feelings aren't everything. They don't run the show.

Moreover, feelings aren't always reliable or consistent. They change. There was a time when you felt deep love for your spouse. There was a time you couldn't imagine having feelings for another person. That changed, didn't it? It can change back.

Our behavior doesn't need to follow our feelings. The opposite can happen, too. Our feelings can follow our behavior.

A spouse who re-commits to his or her marriage – and who behaves accordingly by ending an extramarital relationship – often finds that feelings of love and friendship for his or her spouse begin to return sooner than expected. After all, the obstacle is now gone.

Once the spouse begins to focus his or her efforts and energy back on the spouse and away from the other person, positive emotions for that spouse are often not far behind.

Sometimes, we need to make a decision: Do we do what we know is right, or do we follow our feelings? Sometimes, doing what is right turns out to be in our best interests.

When we are patient with our children, even when they're driving us nuts, they love and respect us more as parents. When we help a friend, even when we're lazy and they're demanding, we nourish a life-long friendship that is there for us in our dark times.

When we re-commit to our spouse and marriage, we give ourselves the chance to be one of those "we made it" couples who get to look back at life with no regrets.

We get to be one of those old couples walking hand-in-hand along the beach, looking back with pride at having overcome our problems and kept our promises. We get to have the love, admiration and respect of our children and grandchildren.

To be sure, there are cases where a marriage has been so awful that it is in the best interests of the spouse (and any children) to leave. Such splits are motivated by the need for physical and emotional well-being, rather than by the allure of a new lover.

Cases that involve abuse or intimidation, high-conflict personalities, untreated mental illness or addiction stand apart. In such instances, the priority isn't saving the marriage – it's staying safe, getting out and getting help.

Ending The Extramarital Relationship & Contact With The Other Person

Let's assume you've decided to re-commit to your spouse, rebuild trust and save your marriage; however, your extramarital partner or friend either doesn't yet know this or is resisting your choice.

Once you have decided to end the extramarital relationship, it is essential that you do so quickly, clearly and completely. You do not owe this other person an explanation.

They know exactly why you are ending it – you are married. Talk about obvious.

There is no reason to meet your extramarital partner in person to find "closure" or let them down easy.

This person has taken more than enough time, energy and emotion away from your spouse, marriage and family.

The moment you decide to wholeheartedly re-commit to your spouse is the moment that the other person must become completely irrelevant in your life.

There can be no further contact of a personal nature. Your attitude and focus must do a complete 180° as you turn from the other person to your spouse.

This is where some unfaithful spouses will waffle, become indignant or even defend the other person. They might say, "It's not her fault, she's a nice girl. She just got caught up in this." Or "He was there when I needed him...I won't be so awful to him."

If that's what you're thinking, you need to get your priorities straight. That might sound harsh. **But know this: The manner in which you end your relationship with the other person can make or break any chance you have of reclaiming your spouse's trust and saving your marriage.**

As I've said from the beginning, a half-hearted attempt to save a marriage is worse than no attempt at all.

I've seen too many cases where a spouse who was carrying on an affair or an opposite-sex friendship had promised to "end it," but nonetheless continued to either initiate contact with, or receive contact from, the other person.

If you're doing this, you need to ask yourself why. Do you still have feelings for the other person? (If so, you should re-read the Should You Always Follow Your Feelings? heading).

Are you reluctant to lose the excitement of engaging with the other person? Are you hesitant to give up the idea and rush of having two people competing for your affection?

If so, I hope you will do some soul-searching and see these motives for what they might be: self-indulgent behaviors that are putting your spouse through hell.

Are you fearful that the other person will damage your career or reputation? If so, talk to your spouse about working as a team to brainstorm ways to limit further fallout from the infidelity.

If your spouse knows that the other person has his or her walking papers, he or she may be willing to make that person's exit as uneventful as possible.

Are you concerned that the other person may harm himself or herself? If so, contact one of his or her friends or family members and leave the problem with them.

After all, what's your alternative? To be manipulated by a person with mental health issues and lose your spouse and possibly family in the process? The other person is not your responsibility.

Keep in mind that when you continue to reach out to, or receive contact from, the other person, your spouse experiences even stronger feelings of anger and of being deceived, abandoned, unloved and disrespected. You are making the situation much worse with every passing moment and each mixed message.

Whatever damage was caused by the affair or inappropriate friendship pales in comparison to your perceived insincerity and flip-flopping. End it hard and fast. Once and for all.

But what about those situations – especially co-worker situations – where ongoing contact is going to happen?

In such cases, it is wise to arrange your job duties in a way that limits interactions in the workplace, and to assure your spouse that any contact between you and the other person will be work-related only.

If the other person contacts you in a personal capacity, let your partner know as soon as possible. Be sure to send an immediate reply telling the other person you will no longer be communicating in a personal way. Let your spouse read this reply.

Remember, when you are gone all day to work, your spouse cannot see you and doesn't know what you're doing. If you've already given that spouse cause to question your trustworthiness, it is natural that his or her mind is going to wander.

This can lead to assumption, accusation and hard feelings as a betrayed spouse says, *"How do I know you weren't flirting with him all day?"* or *"For all I know, you took her out for lunch!"*

Too often, a spouse who has broken his or her partner's trust will lose patience with this line of accusation by saying, *"I've done everything you wanted me to do! What do you want me to do, quit my job? You need to get over it and drop it!"*

Know this: An unfaithful spouse who loses patience with a spouse's feelings of betrayal, insecurity, fear and resentment doesn't just make the situation worse, he or she prolongs and deepens feelings of betrayal, insecurity, fear and resentment.

If you have broken your spouse's trust, it is unwise in the extreme to show impatience or anger or judgment toward your spouse's healing process.

The more you can reassure your spouse, the more you can acknowledge the role you played, and the more patience and love you can show during your spouse's healing process, the faster both of you will be able to get past the affair and get on with life.

"Do I Have To *Prove* That I Ended It?"

Don't be surprised if your spouse asks for "proof" that you have ended the extramarital relationship and severed contact. He or she may need that kind of gesture, especially if you initially resisted ending it or were dishonest about ongoing communication.

Your spouse may need to see that you are willing to choose and prioritize him or her over the other person, without hesitation, qualification or reservation.

Your spouse may need to know that your relationship with the other person means nothing next to your own marriage. Some spouses will say, "After everything you've put me through, it's the least you can do."   That sentiment is surely an understandable one.

Below are some of the actions that your spouse may ask you to take:

- Call, text message or email the other person to say that the relationship is over and that you are rebuilding your marriage. Make it clear that no further contact will be made or replied to.

- Delete the other person's contact information and block that person's phone number / email.

- Get a new phone number or change your email address.

- Delete or suspend social media and other online accounts.

- Re-arrange your social activities to limit contact with the other person (i.e. change gyms, stop frequenting a coffee bar).

- Sever friendships with people who encouraged or enabled the extramarital relationship to continue.

- Re-arrange your business affairs to limit contact with the other person.

- Request a work transfer to a different department or even a different city.

- Request new contact information from your employer (i.e. work email address, work cellphone number).

- Look for a different job.

- Relocate to a new town or city.

If your spouse asks these things of you, try to distinguish between what might be a true inconvenience (i.e. looking for a new job, relocating) versus something that you'd just simply rather not do because it's awkward or troublesome (i.e. getting a new phone number, sending the other person a text to end the relationship).

Whatever you do, do not become indignant or imply that your spouse is paranoid, controlling or unreasonable. Do not tell your spouse that he or she needs to get over it.

Remember: Empathy. Humility. Patience.

The best way you can handle ending the extramarital relationship is by taking the lead. Sever all contact and re-arrange your personal and professional affairs without your spouse having to ask you to do so. Prove that the affair is over.

Do what you know in your heart your spouse would want you to do. Do what you know is in the best interests of your marriage.

Review the previous list. Which of these steps can you take, on your own, to prove to your spouse that the relationship is over? Actions speak louder than words. Your spouse knows that.

Whenever I talk about this issue, I am reminded of a couple I once saw where the wife had had a sexual affair with a much younger personal trainer at the gym she attended.

After the affair was discovered, she ended it and promised to work on her marriage. She deleted the personal trainer's contact information from her phone and assured her husband that she would no longer communicate with him.

She also promised her husband that she would find a new personal trainer at the gym, which she did; however, her husband was a wreck every time she walked out the door to go to the gym.

He would say, "I know you're going to see him there and I can't stand the thought of the two of you making eyes at each other. How do I know you're not talking to him?"

The entire time his wife was at the gym, the husband would sit and stew, preoccupied with images of his wife's younger lover handing her a towel or a bottle of water.

His fears and insecurities got the better of him, until he imagined the two of them sneaking around a corner for a private embrace or passionate kiss.

Soon, he asked his wife to switch gyms.

She refused outright, saying that she had paid for a two-year membership and there was almost a year remaining. She did not want to pay for services she wasn't using.

Her husband didn't care about the money. To him, the gesture and his peace of mind were of more value.

The issue became a major roadblock to their recovery. The wife said it was unreasonable of her husband to ask that she switch gyms, insisting that he "had to trust her."

The husband, however, felt it was very reasonable to expect his wife, who had been discovered having a sexual relationship with a man at the gym, to switch gyms.

In fact, he had hoped that she would take the initiative to do so, knowing how much the gesture would have meant to him.

In this case, I would have to agree with the husband. What is more valuable – getting your money's worth from a gym membership or giving your betrayed spouse peace of mind and a gesture that speaks to your trustworthiness?

I'd have to go with the latter.

Yet this example illustrates the kind of self-focused "bad attitude" that I find often makes it impossible for spouses to act as allies through a crisis of broken trust and to rebuild a marriage that is stronger and happier for both of them.

In this case, the wife never did "get it." To her, her husband's request that she switch gyms was petty and controlling. She continued to accuse him of only wanting to "punish" her. That is, she managed to make it all about her.

Remember: Humility. Empathy. Patience.

This particular wife had none of those things, and it cost her her marriage. She got to keep her gym membership, though.

Here's another thing to keep in mind. Many spouses who have broken trust will tell their partner, "You have to trust me."

The truth is, they do not have to trust you. And they probably don't trust you. You cannot demand a person's trust, you can only earn it. And you earn it by actions, not words.

If you find yourself saying the words, "You have to trust me," bite your lip. A better message is, "I am sincere and I want to earn back your trust."

I will say it again: the best way you can rebuild trust and start moving ahead is by taking the lead.

End the extramarital relationship and take steps to restrict or limit contact in a pro-active way. That is, do it without your spouse having to ask or suggest.

Some betrayed spouses will not ask you to take any steps to limit contact. This is often because they are waiting to see whether you will do so on your own. They are gauging your sincerity.

Other spouses who have been betrayed feel humiliated and are unwilling to humiliate themselves further by asking a spouse to do what that spouse likely knows he or she should do.

When you take the initiative, you come across as authentic and you show your spouse that he or she is your priority. Do not underestimate the value or impact of doing this. It is one of the most important and effective things you can do to show your spouse that you are serious.

Another benefit of this "take the lead" approach is that it gives you the opportunity to arrange matters in a way that works well for you instead of just fulfilling your spouse's requests or demands. It's a pro-active, not reactive, approach.

By taking the lead, you have a chance to reduce the inconvenience or embarrassment you might suffer in your professional and/or personal life.

Dealing With Big Demands:
Should I Quit My Job?" "Should We Move?"

The more you can take pro-active steps to prove to your spouse that the extramarital relationship is over and that you have done *everything humanly possible* to limit contact to unavoidable situations only, the more likely it is that your spouse will feel reassured.

Nonetheless, there are still cases where, following a workplace affair, a betrayed spouse will insist that his or her partner quit his or her job and look for a new one.

This is easier for some people than others. A waiter or waitress may find it isn't too difficult to find work at another restaurant. His or her income and working conditions may remain largely unchanged.

An oil worker in the middle of a "bust" economy may find it difficult to obtain a new job when work is scarce. Quitting his or her job may mean losing a steady income. It may also mean losing the job security that comes with the seniority he or she has built up with the company over the years.

Of all the issues that can make a couple work against each other as enemies instead of working together as allies, this is one of the most difficult. Why? Because it doesn't just involve emotions – which are complex enough – it also involves the real-world logistics of employment, career goals, and the job market.

As you navigate this issue, you should constantly remind yourself to have humility, empathy and patience.

You may have legitimate concerns about your career and/or finances; however, do not let those concerns express themselves as indifference or frustration toward your spouse's feelings.

If you are dealing with a betrayed spouse who is completely immovable in his or her insistence that you quit your job, you must in the end accept that it is a balancing act.

You must weigh the cost, risk and inconvenience of leaving your current job against the cost, risk and inconvenience of losing your current spouse.

In the case presented here of a waiter or waitress who can find another job without suffering any significant hardship, it is probably preferable to do so. It just isn't worth the fight.

In the case presented here of the oil worker, it's tougher. I sympathize with you and I wish that I could give you some kind of magic rule to follow. But I can't and neither can anyone else.

Just keep this in mind: Betrayed spouses often make these demands when they are looking for proof that the unfaithful spouse prioritizes the marriage over his or her career and the other person.

A spouse who has felt betrayed or otherwise mistreated may want proof that an unfaithful partner is willing to make major sacrifices to save the marriage.

If you can consistently and sincerely send your spouse the message that he or she is your priority, your spouse may become more flexible. Meanwhile, do what you can. Take pro-active steps to end and limit contact with the other person, and make sure to tell your spouse what you have done in this regard.

Let your spouse know that you do not secretly miss or want to be with the other person. Let your spouse know that *you avoid contact with the other person like the plague*, since seeing him or her only reminds you of the mistake you made.

Even if the job market is slow, show your spouse that you are working on your resume and keeping apprised of the job market so you can pounce on something the moment it comes along.

Whatever you do, do not descend into impatience, indignation or somehow imply that your spouse is being unreasonable or paranoid.

Do not say, "You have to trust me." Say instead, "I am sincere and I want to earn back your trust."

Big demands aren't always related to a work situation. A husband who discovers his wife is having an affair with their next-door neighbor may insist on selling the home and buying a new one.

He doesn't care that it's a buyer's market and they're going to lose money on the house. He wants to save his marriage.

A wife who discovers her husband has been having an affair with the owner of the only tavern in a very small town may insist on moving to a different city.

She doesn't care that they were raised in this town and that their extended family resides there. She wants to save her marriage.

Like I said, there is no magic rule and no easy answers to these big demands. My advice stands: You must weigh the cost, risk and inconvenience of leaving your current job/house/city/situation against the cost, risk and inconvenience of losing your current spouse and perhaps your family unit.

Sometimes there's no way around making a big change. Some spouses need it to move forward in a way that gives them peace, comfort and security, and it's non-negotiable to them.

I do know one thing, though. When we have to do something, we can always find a way to make it work. There is always another job, another opportunity, another house, another city. Starting a new endeavor together gives you an opportunity for a fresh start as allies, instead of a rotten ending as enemies.

Don't Make Your Spouse "Compete"
With The Other Woman / Man

One of the most gut-wrenching, soul-sucking experiences a betrayed spouse can undergo is feeling like he or she must compete with another person to "win" his or her own spouse.

Again, you need to do some soul-searching here. If you are making your spouse do this – whether directly or indirectly – why?

We've talked about a few of the reasons that some unfaithful spouses continue to see or contact the other person, even when their partner is aware of the extramarital relationship and is desperate for it to end.

They may have feelings for the other person (remember, feelings don't have to run the show), they may enjoy the rush of excitement from the other person's text messages or voice, or they may like indulging in the illusion of the other person.

In some very unfortunate cases, they may enjoy the idea of two people competing for them. It can be quite the ego boost – although it's often one that backfires. Consider this example.

Janet and Daniel were both doctors in their mid-thirties. They had dated since medical school and had been married now for five years. They both worked at the same hospital and were a great team, medically and personally.

Daniel loved his wife. He also loved the feeling he got from helping others, whether patients, colleagues or friends. It made him feel good about himself. Janet admired this about her husband and would constantly tell him what a great person he was.

Nonetheless, Janet sensed that a distance was forming between them. Although Daniel had always been an affectionate husband, he seemed to be more impatient and less doting lately.

One day during rounds, Daniel forgot his cell phone in a patient's room and Janet picked it up. Almost immediately, a text came in that said, "Can u get away 2-nite?" It was from a nurse who had recently started at the hospital.

That night, a heartbroken Janet confronted Daniel about what she suspected was an affair. He admitted to it immediately, and said that he and the nurse – Vanessa – had been seeing each other for almost three months.

Although Janet demanded that he end the affair, Daniel refused. He said, "I need some time...I don't know how I feel. She needs me. She just got out of an abusive marriage. "

Janet was shell-shocked. "I need you too," she said.

"You're strong," said Daniel. "I love you, but you don't need me like she does...I need some space to think about this."

The next several weeks were agony for Janet. Every time Daniel's phone rang or beeped with a text message, he would leave the room to reply in privacy.

Every time he didn't answer his phone, she assumed the worst. Every time he came home late when his shift had ended hours earlier, she knew they had been together.

Desperate to keep her marriage together, Janet tried to be as attractive as possible to Daniel. She cooked his favorite meals, pretended not to notice when he left the room to text or call his girlfriend, and did her best to pleasure him sexually.

She started to ask him for his advice about her medical cases, trying to show him that she too needed him. She cried on his shoulder and told him that she needed him more than anything.

None of that seemed to make a difference. In fact, it only seemed to make Daniel more "confused" about his feelings and about which woman he wanted to be with.

After another few weeks, Daniel came home after work and slumped into a chair. He said, "It's over between me and Vanessa. I told her I wasn't ready to leave you, and she's been seeing a new cardiologist."

Janet was ecstatic and relieved.

But the feeling didn't last for long. Soon, Janet began to think back to how Daniel had waffled between her and the other woman.

She began to think back to the times she had, in her desperation, let him come home late without asking any questions. She thought back to all the times she had cooked a meal or planned a special night, only to have him be a no-show.

She thought back to the emotional turmoil and meltdowns she had gone through, and how he hadn't been there to comfort her – he was with his girlfriend, laughing and pleasuring each other.

She thought back to all the times she had suppressed her own sadness, anxiety and rage while he had sex with his girlfriend and then came home to her, who then also offered him sex.

Looking back, it was becoming crystal-clear to her what had happened. In a state of shock from discovering the affair, she had somehow felt compelled to "compete" with the other woman for Daniel.

She had felt compelled to out-do his girlfriend in all things, hoping that the affair would run its course and he would realize he loved her more.

But the shock was over. Now, all she felt when she looked at Daniel was disgust. Disgust at herself for doing backflips in bed, trying to pleasure him after he had just had sex with his girlfriend. Disgust at how she was probably the laughing stock at work.

And what about his promises to her, the ones about honoring and loving only her? The ones about forsaking all others?

Not only had he broken those, he had dragged her emotions through the mud, indulging his own emotions, pleasure and ego.

She thought of their years together and all the history they shared as a couple. All the good times and bad.

Yet all it took for him to turn away from all of that was some cute nurse with a sob story. Vanessa had played the damsel-in-distress card and Daniel's ego had soaked it up.

If that's how easily he could be manipulated away from her, how could she ever trust him again? If that's how little he valued their marriage, how could she ever love him again? Her resentment grew until she couldn't take it anymore. Enough was enough.

She insisted that Daniel move out of the house, and then told him to find a job at another hospital or she would report him to the medical board for his behavior.

Even if you have true feelings for the extramarital partner or friend, you must realize that continuing with the affair or contact is taking a heart-breaking toll on your spouse.

While you may feel that you have all the control over the situation – after all, it's you that gets to choose, right? – that control is often an illusion. And a temporary one at that.

At some point, your spouse is going to look back at this crisis time in your marriage with the clarity of hindsight. You need to think, right now, about what he or she will see.

Take great care to ensure that your spouse does not feel that he or she must compete with the other person. Do not allow him or her to contact the other person or do anything else that might chip away at his or her dignity.

Such things have a way of coming back to haunt a spouse and to destroy a relationship that might otherwise have thrived.

If your genuine goal is to rebuild trust and repair your marriage, you must begin to make your spouse feel that he or she is the most important person in your life.

That has to happen even if you have legitimate complaints about your spouse or the marriage. Why? Because most married people have legitimate complaints about each other at some time.

But the way to resolve those problems is by working together as a team of two, not by bringing another player onto the field and ignoring all the rules.

Inappropriate Opposite-Sex Friendships

Of course, there are certainly cases where a spouse misinterprets or mistakenly assumes the worst about an opposite-sex friendship that his or her spouse is having.

It may be an innocent mistake or it may be due to a particularly insecure, jealous or controlling personality. It may be because that person experienced a breach of trust in the past.

But if the situation is serious enough that you're reading this book, we're going to operate under the assumption that there was more to it.

In my professional experience, many if not most spouses who suspect their spouse is having an "inappropriate" opposite-sex friendship unfortunately do have cause for concern. These friendships often warp into emotional and physical affairs.

Yet when asked to end an opposite-sex friendship, many spouses become indignant and refuse. Instead, they turn the situation around by blaming their spouse's insecurity.

They might say, *"You're crazy, we're just friends"* or *"you're paranoid"* or *"we just talk about work, get over it!"* or *"I'm not going to end a friendship just because you're being unreasonable."*

This leaves suspicious spouses in an even greater state of feeling betrayed, unheard, devalued and disrespected. They know there's more to it. They aren't stupid. But at the same time, they are powerless. Every time they try to talk about it, they are meant to feel like a "jealous wife" or a "jealous husband."

Be brutally honest with yourself: Have you been doing this to your spouse? If so, why? Do you enjoy the emotional arousal or sense of friendship you get by communicating with the other person? If so, you're not alone.

Almost all inappropriate opposite-sex friendships involve an element of friendship and sexual attraction, held slightly at bay, which in itself can add to their appeal.

Ask yourself: How did or does my use of personal technology (i.e. text messaging, social media, etc.) factor into this?

As we get further into this part of the book, I will give you some strategies to communicate all of this to your spouse so that you can work together to move past them.

But for now, I want you to think about the importance of acknowledging your spouse's feelings instead of downplaying them or making him or her feel "crazy, " "pathetic," or "jealous."

Remember: Empathy. Humility. Patience.

If you know in your heart that your spouse was right about the opposite-sex friendship – that all or part of it was inappropriate – tell your spouse that. Doing so doesn't make you look guilty. It makes you look honest and sincere in your attempts to rebuild trust and prioritize your spouse, not the other person.

Again, If your genuine goal is to rebuild trust and repair your marriage, you must begin to make your spouse feel that he or she is the most important person in your life.

Online Activity & Indiscretions

As with inappropriate friendships, spouses may disagree over whether an online activity or indiscretion – perhaps a profile on a dating site or sex chat with a stranger – is actual infidelity.

My advice stands: instead of arguing over the definition of cheating, it is more productive to agree that "trust has been broken" in the marriage.

At the very least, that much consensus is necessary to move forward. It allows the betrayed spouse to feel that his or her concerns are being taken seriously, while simultaneously letting the offending spouse maintain some dignity. After all, it can be embarrassing to have one's personal Internet habits exposed, especially if they are of a sexual nature.

Many spouses – men and women – who are happily married will engage in some extent of online sexual activity, such as occasionally viewing Internet porn or reading online erotica.

In most instances, the activity does not compromise the relationship. In fact, some spouses engage in this as a way to spark arousal for lovemaking.

In this way, the activity can enhance or maintain sexual and emotional intimacy. Online sexual activity is present, but the relationship is always prioritized.

However, problems arise when a spouse engages in activity that becomes compulsive or habitual, or that takes time, energy and intimacy away from his or her spouse. The activity is prioritized over the relationship.

Problems also arise when the activity involves interaction with a "real" person, even a stranger.

Sex chat, online dating profiles that send and receive messages, and live-streaming, interactive pornography are examples of activities that a spouse may feel violate the privacy that should exist within marriage.

It is reasonable to say that online activity – whether sexual on not – that compromises or negatively impacts a person's relationship with his or her spouse is a problem that needs to be addressed in the marriage.

For example, if your spouse spent excessive time, money or energy online instead of with you in "the real world," you would likely resent that.

It may be that your spouse *does* in fact spend too much time online or on social media, and that you are bothered by it.

That might actually be helpful. It gives the two of you a shared complaint that might make it easier to collaborate and reduce the time each of you spends online.

As many of us know, the Internet can be extremely habit-forming. It doesn't matter what we're looking up – funny cat videos, movie trailers, useless trivia, celebrity news – it's all too easy to lose ourselves for hours in an Internet "shame spiral" of pointless surfing.

Social media is particularly habit-forming as we feel compelled, for some unknown reason, to know what is happening in the lives of friends and strangers alike, and to tell them what is happening in ours.

Now add the thrill of erotic excitement and instant sexual gratification to this magnetic mix.

The allure of going online to engage in sex chat, toy with voyeuristic sexual relations or watch pornography can become even more compelling, compulsive and distracting.

More and more, we are seeing quality research being done into the effects of online addiction, both sexual and non-sexual. This book is not an exhaustive study on the topic.

Rather, the goal here will be to identify whether this is a problem in your marriage and to offer some practical ideas to move past it.

For most people, this will be enough; however, if you feel you are truly "addicted" to online sexual activity, including porn, professional in-person therapy from a mental health practitioner who specializes in this uniquely challenging area may be required to help you resolve this issue, rebuild trust, and repair your marriage.

If your spouse has confronted you with knowledge of your sex-related Internet habits, you may be feeling a wave of various emotions.

You may be embarrassed and angry and, if your spouse found this information by stumbling upon it or by looking for it on your computer, you may feel that your privacy has been violated.

Indeed, your spouse may also be feeling that his or her privacy has been violated, especially if he or she has come across secret communications or sexual interactions between you and another person.

Your spouse may be angry that you have been devoting time to this person or activity instead of to the marriage.

While it's understandable if you are angry – particularly if your spouse "went digging" for this content – I encourage you to ask yourself what compelled him or her to take such actions.

I'm not excusing or defending those actions – I'm just asking you to think about why your spouse did it.

Was it to humiliate you? Was it to control you?

Or was it to confirm suspicions that he or she had, suspicions that stemmed from a lack of emotional or sexual intimacy between you?

Was it to try to understand why you have been spending so much time on the computer instead of with him or her?

Was your spouse's motivation based on cruelty and control? Or was it based on concern and a desire to understand why there has been distance between the two of you?

Answering these questions may help your feelings of anger or indignation dissipate, so that you and your spouse can begin to rebuild the trust and happiness in your marriage.

You will also have to ask yourself why you engaged in the online activity.

Was it out of boredom? Was it because of a lack of sexual intimacy in your marriage? Did it start as a harmless "kick" that became more habitual?

Again, there are strategies later in this part of the book that can help you and your spouse talk about this issue in a purposeful and respectful way.

Regardless, if your goal is to rebuild trust and intimacy in your marriage, it is likely that you will have to curtail your online sexual activity in a practical way.

Many habitual online behaviors, including porn and other activities of a sexual nature, develop for three reasons:

a) boredom
b) ease of access
c) instant gratification

Not only can Internet activity of a sexual nature add a little excitement to one's day (or night), but it is easily and widely accessible.

A few keystrokes and anything you want you see is right before your eyes. Sexual gratification is immediate and requires no effort on your part.

If you are willing to work with your partner to move past this problem, brainstorm ways that you can change your lifestyle habits so that you can "break the pattern" of engaging in this activity at certain predictable points in your day or evening.

For example, if it was your habit to go online after dinner, suggest that you and your spouse do something together after dinner to distract you and break the habit.

You may also want to brainstorm ways you can make Internet access more of a challenge, whether it is giving the password to the Wi-Fi or computer to your spouse or putting stricter controls on your computer.

Turn to your spouse. Even if she is or he is angry, express your sincere desire to restore your emotional and physical intimacy.

Ask your partner to work with you on this, as allies.

At the same time, take the initiative to show that you are serious about moving past this issue, whether it is by deleting online profiles or merging your and your spouse's social media accounts.

Building A Fortress Around Your Marriage

Whether your marriage is struggling with the strain of a full-blown sexual or emotional affair, an online or other indiscretion, or an inappropriate opposite-sex friendship, it is essential that you and your spouse begin to feel "protective" of your marriage.

Strong marriages do have a fortress of sorts around them. In fact, it can be helpful to use this metaphor to discuss privacy in your marriage in a larger sense.

This fortress embraces the couple and any children they have. Its walls keep feelings of love, friendship, devotion and happiness in.

The walls of this fortress also keep destructive forces out. That includes other people who could in some way "chip away" at the marriage, including nosey in-laws, negative family members, judgmental or opposite-sex friends and extramarital lovers.

Seeing your marriage in this way can summon positive feelings of protectiveness. It can even change the way a person thinks about an opposite-sex friend or affair partner.

Instead of this person being a friend or confidante, he or she becomes an intruder and an enemy. Instead of defending the extramarital relationship, a spouse feels more compelled to defend the marriage and family unit.

In keeping with this marital fortress of love, devotion, solidarity and privacy, you should be careful and selective when choosing the people you will talk to about the infidelity in your marriage.

Like it or not, your marriage problems may be nothing more than amusing gossip to some of your friends.

Your friends and family members may be unduly influenced by their own negative feelings, experiences or agendas and this in turn may influence you.

Ideally, spouses should agree on the friends or family members that they can each turn to as confidantes. You are dealing with enough feelings of betrayal in your marriage. Don't add to them by talking to someone your partner doesn't trust.

Unfortunately, you may have to reveal your personal situation to some people you wouldn't normally confide in.

For example, if the infidelity or inappropriate opposite-sex friendship was with a co-worker, you may have to inform a superior to arrange transfer to another department or to otherwise limit contact with the other person.

If the affair was with a family friend, you may have to tell certain family members or friends to ensure that you don't bump into the other person at social events.

Commit To Restoring Trust & Building A Fortress Around Your Marriage

Do you like those big-budget disaster movies? I love them. They're escapist and fun. I love the spectacle of alien invasions blowing up military strongholds and political epicenters.

I love the way everybody raids the grocery stores for essential water and food, and then stuffs their station wagons and SUV's with supplies.

They grab their kids (and maybe the family golden retriever, for the *awww* effect) and race off toward the highway, looking for a safe place to hunker down and hide.

I remember back in 2012 when pop culture and some wonky interpretation of the Mayan calendar had predicted the end of the world. There was a big-budget disaster movie that came out – called *2012* – that featured a broken family unit caught in the chaos of the impending apocalypse.

The former couple had two children, who lived with the mother and her new boyfriend. The father resided elsewhere; however, when the skies started darkening and the shit really started to hit the fan – guess what?

The couple instinctively turn toward each other to protect their children, and the love between them was rekindled.

Cheesy? Tacky? Oh, I hope you don't think so. The truth is, it sometimes takes a crisis to make us get our priorities straight and to make us realize what really matters to us.

It sometimes takes an apocalyptic event to make us realize how short-sighted and self-focused we have been, and how we need to start protecting the things that are most valuable to us.

That's what building a fortress around your marriage or relationship is all about.

I've seen first-hand the effects of divorce and family breakdown. I've seen how short-sighted people can be.

When faced with a problem, they fail to think long-term. Instead, they focus on their current feelings: frustration, anger, betrayal, sadness, resentment and so on.

They see their spouse as someone who is standing in the way of their short-term happiness, rather than as someone who has the potential to bring long-term happiness to their life.

Instead of working together as allies to build and maintain a fortress around their marriage and/or family life, they work against each other as enemies to tear the fortress apart from within.

Let me ask you: What do you think your life will look like in five years from now if you do not work with your spouse to rebuild trust and save your marriage?

Be realistic. Too often, people assume the path to happiness, fulfillment and true, perfect love will open up like flower in May once the divorce papers are signed.

Yet as often as not, they find life post-divorce isn't as sunny as they imagined. New partners often come with a lot of baggage, including their own trail of failed relationships and perhaps a few bratty and spoiled kids for good measure.

The grass isn't always greener on the other side of the fence. Frankly, it often has a lot more weeds – although they're only visible once you've hopped the fence to have a closer look.

Moreover, your ex-spouse probably won't remain single for long. If you have children, that means that you will lose a certain amount of say and control over the people that are waltzing in and out of the lives of your kids. You will have little or no control over the person that your ex-spouse begins to sleep with, bring into the home and expose to your children on a daily and/or nightly basis.

Plus, kids don't stay little forever. When they're older, they may ask you why you didn't try harder to make the marriage work.

How will you answer them when they are adults with minds of their own, not children who are easily swayed by padded answers or a trip to the toy store?

Think long-term – for yourself, your spouse and any kids.

None of this is meant to be sermonizing. It isn't a scare tactic. Rather, it's a reality check. Relationship and/or family breakdown often have consequences that people don't anticipate.

The truth is, there is great pride in keeping a marriage and family together. It's something too few people and couples get to feel nowadays.

You're an adult and you can make your own decisions. I only encourage you to think about that fortress. If the skies started to fall, if the zombie apocalypse began this moment, who would you instinctively grab and protect, with your life if need be, within the walls of that fortress?

Let's recap where we are at this point: You've acknowledged the fact that you've broken your spouse's trust, and you've exercised empathy, humility and patience. Your spouse knows the type and extent of the extramarital relationship, as well as the other person's identity.

You've ended the relationship with the other person and restricted contact to only what is absolutely essential or unavoidable. Maybe you've even agreed to a major change, such as looking for a new job or relocating to a new house or city.

You've told the people who need to know and taken other initial steps, such as re-structuring your online presence, deleting problematic email or online accounts, or suspending or uniting social media accounts.

Now what? Well, now you're ready to really get to work. Now you're ready to rebuild the fortress around your marriage and family, brick by brick, by working as allies and not enemies.

Now you're ready to move on to the more significant steps you must take to move forward, re-establish trust, understand why it all happened and ultimately prevent it from happening again.

Be An Open Book

The fortress around a strong marriage is rock-solid when seen from the outside. No one can see through the walls. It's hard to know what's happening inside.

And that's a good thing since, most of the time, it's no one else's business.

Inside the walls of the fortress, however, the view is crystal clear. Spouses can see everything. There is total transparency. Nothing is hidden.

And never is this transparency more important than in the weeks and months following a breach in trust.

Spouses who are struggling to rebuild after infidelity should agree to leave smartphones and computers unlocked and accessible by the other partner. They should agree to share passwords to all electronics and social media and other online accounts.

It is counter-productive to demand that only the unfaithful spouse provides this level of transparency. Yes, he or she is the one who broke trust; however, if you want to have a strong fortress around your marriage, both spouses have to play by the same rules.

Mutual transparency within marriage is one of the smartest, most practical things you can do to resolve a breach of trust and prevent future breaches from happening.

Some people may say that personal electronics and accounts are "private." If you and your spouse both agree on that approach and are comfortable with it, then great. Go with it.

But if your spouse prefers an "open book" policy and you don't – and you're the one who has broken trust – it is unreasonable to expect your spouse to be okay with private passwords and locked devices.

There's a saying: *Those who have nothing to hide, hide nothing*. In the wake of an affair, online indiscretion or inappropriate friendship, your spouse will be living by that motto.

None of this means that your spouse has a perpetual license to check your smartphone, computer or online accounts as a habit or as a way to punish or control you to the grave.

As time goes on and your spouse's feelings of betrayal and suspicion subside, the frequency with which he or she scrolls through your text messages or checks your online activity should naturally decrease.

That's good, since even a well-meaning spouse, one who has broken trust but is committed to rebuilding and to transparency, can grow weary of constantly being checked up on in this way.

Resist the urge to roll your eyes or sigh with irritation when your spouse checks your phone or computer. And do not, no matter what, say "You need to get over it already!" or "You're paranoid!"

Remember: Empathy. Humility. Patience.

Also, know this. In the other part of this book – the part your spouse is reading – I have warned betrayed spouses about the dangers of checking a partner's phone obsessively or too often.

I have explained that this behavior can be highly irritating, even to a spouse who is eager to restore trust and work toward a happier, stronger marriage.

That being the case, there's no need for you to criticize your spouse for this behavior or complain about it. That will only be counter-productive.

Instead, realize that that seed of knowledge has been planted. Focus less on your spouse's actions and more on what you need to do to move forward.

The Gory Details

Spouses who have had their trust broken by a partner's sexual affair vary widely in terms of the "details" they want to know or hear. Some won't want to hear anything.

Others will ask the basics – who, what, why, how long, etc. – but won't want to hear explicit details that might burn permanent images into their brain. Still others will want to know everything. They will ask about how many times you had sex, in what positions, whether there was oral or anal sex involved and how many times you had an orgasm or gave the other person an orgasm.

They will ask about the other woman's breasts and how tight she was. They will ask about how big the other man's penis was and whether he lasted longer.

These kinds of explicit Question & Answer periods aren't just excruciating for the betrayed partner, they can be humiliating for the unfaithful partner on many levels.

When your spouse is firing questions at you about these kinds of gory details, he or she is saying, *"I am terrified that you enjoyed him / her more than me…I am terrified that we will never again be intimate without you fantasizing about him / her…I am terrified that deep down you really want him / her more than me, and that you're only staying with me because you have to…"*

As much as possible, try to steer clear of providing explicit details that you know will hurt your spouse.

Instead, focus on reassuring him or her that the extramarital partner was not as satisfying, pleasurable or desirable as your spouse – and that goes for both in bed and out.

Send the message that the illusion of the other person was much better than the reality.

Focus on reassuring your spouse that the encounters you had with the other person were unfulfilling and often awkward and that nothing compares to the lovemaking between the two of you.

In the other part of this book – the part your spouse is reading – I have warned betrayed spouses about the dangers of hearing the gory details. Once he or she has heard something, it cannot be unheard.

For your part, I would encourage you to send your spouse the message that the sooner you can remove all memory of the other person from your mind, the better.

Let your spouse know that summoning memories of the other person is a painful experience for you, not because you miss the other person but because you desperately want to forget that person ever existed. That's what your spouse wants to hear.

Getting Back In Sync With Each Other: From Children to Chores

Once the initial ground-work of rebuilding trust has been done (i.e. the extramarital relationship and contact has ended, your spouse knows the essential facts, you've agreed on transparency, etc.), you and your spouse should try to get back in sync with each other. Getting back into the swing of normal life can help.

This is especially so if you have children. To them, it should be "business as usual" as soon as possible. Infidelity is an issue that most adults have great difficulty understanding and coping with – so you can imagine how it affects a child.

While it may be necessary and wise to let your children know that "mom and dad" are facing a problem, the message should be that you are facing it together, for the most part behind closed doors.

Let your kids see that you and your partner are facing life's problems as a team. As allies, not enemies.

Your kids must know that no matter what happens, their parents will continue to be in their lives and will continue to co-parent in a way that shows respect to each other.

As parents, you know your children best. You know their personalities, maturity levels, fears and strengths. You know what they can handle for their age.

Just don't overestimate what they can handle. An older child who asks, "What's wrong, Dad? What can I do?" is doing so out of love, fear and concern.

Do not assume that child is capable of being your confidante or counselor, and do not divulge unpleasant details to them. Do not let your child "parent" you. They are living with enough stress.

Never unload your guilt on your children or use them to make inroads with the other parent by saying, "I feel so awful about all of this...can you tell your mom / dad how sorry I am?"

Do not say, "I am trying hard to get your mom / dad to forgive me, but she / he just won't." Not only is that unfair, your spouse will recognize it as manipulation and you will only make matters worse.

Do not ever suggest to your children that this situation is in any way the fault of their other parent, or that the other parent isn't as invested in repairing the marriage as you are.

Instead, show your children that you and your spouse are working as allies to build a fortress not just around each other, but around them, too. Actions speak louder than words.

Despite the stress and emotion that descends on a household during a crisis of broken trust, life must go on.

You and your spouse should commit to working together to ensure the day-to-day demands of daily life are met.

This can be a challenge when emotions are high. You and/or your spouse may find yourselves becoming quickly irritated, insulted or hurt by even the most innocent or well-meaning of actions or statements. You might be quick to anger, break into tears or jump to negative conclusions.

For example, I've seen couples who were making real progress suddenly lose ground and descend into conflict over something as seemingly insignificant as a sink full of dirty dishes.

I've seen couples who had rebuilt significant trust suddenly fall into fear, suspicion and assumption because of a dead battery in a cell phone and a check-in phone call that came ten minutes later than a spouse expected it would.

My point is this: you and your spouse should be clear about what you expect of each other in terms of housework, the kids, paying bills, socializing, checking-in with each other and so on.

Do not assume that your spouse will have the same expectations as you. He or she probably won't. This is not the time for mind-reading.

Talking About It:
Phase I & Phase II

In my experience, many couples who find themselves reeling from the discovery of an affair, indiscretion or inappropriate friendship are too quick to "talk about it" for hours, days, weeks on end.

Despite the intense anger, sadness, fear and other often unpredictable and conflicting emotions and assumptions that attend infidelity, too many couples launch into this kind of discussion without any kind of structure or plan.

They just start talking. And then guess what? They usually start fighting. It's almost inevitable.

I always recommend a two-phase approach when talking about and coping with infidelity. This helps bring some structure to an otherwise chaotic discussion, and moves the conversation ahead in a purposeful, not emotional or impulsive, way.

Don't underestimate the value of structure and patience. After all, this breach of trust may be the most important thing that you and your spouse ever talk about in your lives.

In the immediate aftermath of a discovered infidelity, certain facts need to be known and certain actions need to be taken. This is phase I, the stabilizing phase, and it includes the kinds of things that you've read so far, including:

- The identity of the other person

- Was the infidelity emotional, sexual or tech-based

- Whether the extramarital relationship has ended

- Whether contact between them has ended

- Agreeing on transparency (i.e. shared passwords, etc.)

- Establishing a mutual commitment to work on the marriage and build a fortress of love and privacy around it

- Establishing normalcy in the home by discussing how to deal with the kids, check-in with each other, share housework, etc.

This is how I think of this initial phase: Imagine a gunshot victim being rushed into the emergency room of a hospital. He is in shock and his vital signs are weakening by the moment.

Of course, the bullet needs to be removed. But before the patient has the strength to survive the operation, his condition must be stabilized.

X-rays must be taken to show where the bullet is. Once that happens, he can survive the process – the operation – that must happen if his life is to be saved.

It's the same thing with infidelity. In the wake of an infidelity, both spouses are in shock. The betrayed spouse is in the shock of discovery while the unfaithful spouse is in the shock of being found out.

Before these spouses can survive the process of rebuilding trust and saving their marriage, they must stabilize their life and situation. They must know the basic facts of the matter and arrange their lives in a way that will support them as they move forward.

And again, that's what you've done until this point.

If phase I is the stabilizing phase, then phase II – which is where you are now – is what we can think of as the recovery and prevention phase.

Now, it's time to dig a little deeper and to find out why the infidelity happened. What made the marriage vulnerable to it? How did each spouse contribute to it? How can a couple make sure it doesn't happen again?

These questions take longer to answer. They require a long-term commitment, self-reflection, humility, great love for our spouse and a willingness to change one's behavior, outlook and perhaps even priorities.

Of course, a couple who is struggling to rebuild trust and strengthen their marriage will have to talk through their problems and pain to find insight and solutions.

My goal, however, is to make each discussion as purposeful as possible thus reducing the overall number of conversations that are necessary.

Why? Because a couple who keeps talking about it indefinitely, who keeps bringing it up and reliving all the pain that goes with it, will never move past it.

Instead, they will experience regular feelings of anger, betrayal and resentment toward each other, feelings that will eventually settle into a sense of hopelessness about the marriage.

They will begin to think that nothing will ever change. It will never get better. And when couples begin to feel that sense of futility, they tend to "give up."

The Heart-To-Heart: Communication Tips

Let's run through some initial things to keep in mind as you and your spouse begin to engage in heart-to-heart discussions about the infidelity or indiscretion, including why it happened.

• **Timing.** Couples often underestimate the importance of good timing. If your spouse has just walked through the door after a long, unpleasant day at work, it won't be helpful to rush up to him and her and say, "We need to talk right now!" He or she might otherwise be open to the conversation; however, the timing is all wrong and he or she is likely to react with irritation.

Instead, put thought into when you will discuss the issue. In some cases, it is best to schedule a conversation so that spouses can mentally prepare and take steps to limit distractions, such as being interrupted by the kids, phone calls or unexpected visitors.

In other cases, spontaneous conversations can work well, especially if the couple is feeling loving, open-minded and cooperative. Use your own judgment – just think before you speak.

- **Environment.** Arguments and conflict often have a predictable nature to them. Many couples will say that they have the same fight, at the same time, in the place, almost all the time.

To break out of this predictable pattern, think about how you can change your environment so that it contributes to the atmosphere of the conversation in a positive, not negative, way.

I have actually advised some couples to "get away from it all" and spend a night or two in a hotel – even a local one – so that they can talk about their problems against a different background. This in itself can be helpful.

Perhaps even better, you can ask your spouse to take an evening "walk and talk." You can walk hand-in-hand, moving forward – literally and symbolically – as you have a heart-to-heart conversation. The invigorating night air, the starry sky and the physical exertion can soothe emotions and keep them in check. This is a great evening ritual to rebuild affection and friendship.

• **Mood.** In addition to timing and environment, it is important to set a "good mood," one that facilitates an honest and positive conversation.

Talking by candlelight, playing soft music or even sitting in a hot-tub can all relax the spirit and open the heart.

Humor can help, too. I have suggested that clients watch something funny (i.e. "fail" videos, a favorite comedy or sitcom, etc.) before a serious conversation and to even take "time outs" during that conversation to find solace and perspective in laughter.

The point is not to trivialize the infidelity. The point is to balance a heavy conversation with a lighter tone so that the discussion does not turn into a destructive, hateful one.

A couple who is working through infidelity must learn to tackle all their problems in a way that strengthens, not weakens, the marriage.

• **Your attitude.** Go back and read the heading earlier in this part called Attitude Adjustments. Remember: Empathy. Humility. Patience.

Even though you are the spouse who broke trust, you may have legitimate complaints about your partner and your marriage. You may be eager to talk about your needs and what you would like to see your spouse do differently moving forward.

Despite your own remorse, you might be fed up with your spouse's nasty voice tone, critical nature or lack of affection. To be happy in the marriage, these things will have to improve.

That's fair enough. You will have an opportunity to express yourself in this way as we move through the next few subheadings. Just keep in mind that you must at all times remain accountable for your actions.

Do not ever imply that your spouse was to blame for your affair, indiscretion or inappropriate friendship. Do not ever roll your eyes or send your spouse the message that he or she needs to "get over it."

The more you can keep a loving, patient and humble attitude, the more receptive your spouse is going to be to the complaints you have about the marriage and to the changes in behavior that you may want to ask of him or her.

● **Voice tone.** Make sure that your voice tone stays positive, pleasant and cooperative. An angry, impatient or defensive voice tone will sabotage any efforts to move forward.

● **Humility.** We live in a society that is becoming increasingly narcissistic and self-focused. We are very good at expressing our own feelings and complaints, but tend to rise up in defensiveness or indignation when someone else does the same.

Be sure to regularly "self-check" your attitude so that your spouse gets the message that you care about his or her happiness and what he or she has to say.

Spend less time defending yourself or trying to prove how you were "right" and how your spouse was "wrong," and spend more time trying to understand and empathize with your spouse's perspective. That will get you much further.

• **Emotional control.** Not only am I seeing more self-focused clients these days, I'm also seeing more clients who erupt into what can only be described as adult temper-tantrums.

We all lose our cool from time to time and emotional outbursts are to be expected as spouses navigate something as bumpy as infidelity.

Spouses should know their own and each other's "triggers" so they can work together to manage them.

That is, what emotions tend to trigger your and/or your spouse's outbursts?

Common emotional triggers include feelings of being unappreciated, unheard, unloved, undesirable, fearful, misunderstood, rejected or not prioritized.

But there's a difference between an occasional meltdown and regular explosions of blind rage, especially if that rage is very easily triggered or accompanied by physically aggressive behavior.

If you or your spouse displays short-fuse or "hair trigger" behavior, and you're unable to control it by yourself or by working as a team, I recommend seeking in-person professional help from a mental health practitioner who specializes in anger management. This is a growing and important area of specialization that can help.

- **Emotional oversensitivity.** It isn't just emotional outbursts that can be a barrier to effective communication. Emotional withdrawal or super-sensitivity can also stand in the way.

No one likes to get their feelings hurt; however, a spouse who retreats into wounded silence or bursts into tears whenever their behavior is challenged – even gently so – makes it impossible for their partner to express legitimate complaints.

Self-check yourself for this behavior. If your feelings are "easily bruised" and you are using this to either suppress your partner's complaints or avoid having to respond to them in a straightforward manner, you are causing great damage to your relationship. And whether you realize it or not, you are likely causing your partner to feel very resentful toward you.

Just like the person who "blows up" when faced with a criticism, you may succeed in getting your partner to back down and be quiet; however, you're wrong if you think that means the complaints have disappeared. They're still there. They're just bottled up. And inside the bottle, the pressure is growing.

Your partner deserves to have his or her legitimate complaints heard, even if those complaints are hard for you to hear.

If your partner is expressing this behavior, do your best to steer clear of the words that trigger it and always keep a respectful voice tone. Reassure him or her that the purpose of the discussion is to improve the relationship for both of you.

Let your spouse know that you are finding it difficult to say what you need to say, and ask for his or her input – *"What can I do to make the conversation easier for you?"* When he or she does hear you out, show your support and appreciation.

If that doesn't work, you will have to express your own frustrations and feelings of being "controlled" by your partner's oversensitivity. Emotional oversensitivity can be just as controlling and manipulative as emotional outbursts. Some people are fully aware they are doing it, while others haven't considered the impact their oversensitivity has on others.

● **Mind your manners.** In addition to being aware of your voice tone and keeping it respectful, do not interrupt your spouse any more than necessary.

At times it may be necessary to interrupt him or her to clarify something that was said. Just be sure that you aren't interrupting to defend yourself, contradict something your spouse said or to offer unnecessary feedback. People need to feel heard.

Also, watch your body language and ensure it remains respectful and encouraging. Don't roll your eyes, cross your arms in a display of stubbornness or shake your head disapprovingly. The goal is to keep the conversation going, not give someone an excuse to say, "Oh, what's the point? You're not even listening to me."

- **Long-term thinking.** A betrayed spouse often falls into a type of panic mode. There is a sense of urgency: *Tell me everything, now! Are you committed to this marriage? Why did you do it? Talk to me now! How can I ever trust you? We need to fix this, now!*

An unfaithful spouse can also fall into this type of panic mode and feel a similar sense of urgency. He or she might say, *Are you going to be able to forgive me or not? I need to know right now! I can't do this unless I know that you're going to stay.*

Yet as I've said earlier, recovering from infidelity and rebuilding a marriage is a long-term process and your thinking should also be focused on the long-term. Do **not** pressure your spouse to give you a definitive "Yes, I'll stay" or "No, it's over" answer. You can't force someone else to live by your timeline.

There is no magic moment that will mark the end of conflict. There is no magic word you can say that will make your spouse forgive and forget. Instead of seeking a fast, urgent and final solution, it may be wiser to take a more patient approach.

Whether the wound is a physical or emotional one, time does help with the healing process. Instead of seeing time as the enemy, embrace what it has to offer.

"Why Did It Happen?"
Stupid Mistakes, Texting Temptations,
Pre-Existing Problems & More...

Ah, now that's a loaded question and there are countless self-help books, psychological theories and wild speculations as to why trust breaks down in a relationship.

In my professional capacity as a couples mediator, I have seen emotional and sexual affairs, various indiscretions and inappropriate friendships develop for all kinds of reasons. I'm going to outline a handful of the more common reasons here, and in the following two headings.

Do you see traces of your situation in any of these reasons?

• Sometimes, an unfaithful spouse has suffered some kind of past trauma, was a child of divorce or grew up in a particularly dysfunctional family unit that lacked good role models. These challenges can definitely affect our intimate relationships as adults.

• Other people suffer from personality disorders (i.e. narcissism, bi-polarism, etc.) or other challenges (i.e. addiction) which if left unmanaged can make it virtually impossible to enjoy a meaningful, mature and devoted intimate relationship.

● Despite the pain caused and the betrayal involved, an indiscretion – especially a one-time or minor one – can be a "stupid mistake."

It may have been a temporary lapse in judgment that has nothing to do with a spouse's love for his or her partner or overall commitment level to the relationship and/or family unit.

This can be a difficult – even offensive or insulting – message for a betrayed spouse to hear. After all, how can something that hurt him or her so profoundly, and that caused such stress and fear, not have an equally profound reason?

It's human nature – when we feel a serious pain, we assume it is caused by something serious. We naturally seek out a reason that is as "big" as our pain.

Normally, this makes sense – the bigger the blade, the deeper the cut, right? But that logic doesn't always apply when it comes to indiscretions.

Have you ever had a bad paper-cut? They sting like hell, right? Did knowing it was just a piece of paper reduce the level of pain you felt? Of course not.

My point is this: if you believe your indiscretion was a stupid mistake, do not expect your spouse to attribute such slight regard to it. **Even if it "meant nothing" to you, it has caused great pain to your spouse and you must acknowledge that.**

You must also take steps to show your spouse that this mistake will not become a pattern in your marriage.

Imagine being afflicted with a thousand tiny paper-cuts on your hands. Even though each individual cut is tiny, the overall pain is excruciating. That's what happens when those "stupid mistakes" start to add up.

• Infidelity and indiscretions may also happen when couples "slide" into marriage after co-habiting or having children. They got married because it seemed like the next step, not because they actively chose to do so.

Such couples are often very much in love; however, the commitment to marriage wasn't there at the time. An infidelity or indiscretion can often make these couples re-define their relationship in a more deliberate, clear and committed way.

• Quite commonly, infidelity and other forms of broken trust happen when a spouse feels somehow unsatisfied in the marriage and therefore looks outside of it to find the kind of fulfillment or pleasure that he or she needs.

Ongoing emotional or sexual affairs often fall into this category. A wife who feels unloved or unsupported by her husband might turn to a sympathetic male co-worker who befriends her.

A husband who feels unappreciated and sexually rejected by his wife may turn to a female co-worker who seems to admire him.

This kind of "traditional infidelity" is often believed to be a symptom of an already unhealthy marriage. That is, people tend to have affairs or indiscretions when there are pre-existing problems.

The situation is compounded if spouses don't have the communication or interpersonal skills to understand and resolve their problems before they hit a crisis point. They may exist in a relationship that is fraught with mixed messages, negative assumptions and miserable dynamics.

As you work through this part of the book – and particularly as you get to the Questions To Ask Yourself and Questions To Ask Your Spouse headings – you will find strategies to help you and your partner figure out where any pre-existing problems in your relationship might have been.

- We've covered this reason before – technology and temptation. More and more, spouses who are in love with and committed to their spouse and/or family are being drawn into emotional and sexual affairs, online indiscretions and inappropriate friendships that begin via personal technology. I sometimes call these e-affairs or iFriendships.

This type of broken trust is more widespread than you might think and, in my experience, may be becoming the most common type of infidelity that modern couples struggle with.

Since it's unlikely that the growth and development of personal forms of technology is going to slow down, we can expect the rates of tech-based broken trust to continue to rise.

As was covered earlier, personal technology – smartphones, texting, email, social media and so on – make it incredibly easy to get caught up in the "rush" of an emotional or sexual dialogue with another person, whether a friend, colleague or stranger.

This creates a false sense of intimacy between a spouse and another person, one that develops into an extramarital relationship far faster than it otherwise would.

Believe it or not, the "traditional" type of infidelity – where a spouse is unfaithful because something is lacking in the marriage – can be easier to remedy. Because there is an identifiable problem, it is easier to identify and agree upon solutions.

In such cases, the betrayed partner is able to see how his or her behavior contributed to the disconnect in the marriage. That can facilitate a spirit of cooperation and help spouses rebuild trust and make their marriage a happier one for both partners. It is easier to work together when both spouses can accept blame.

That can't always happen with today's e-affairs and iFriendships. But that doesn't mean trust cannot be restored and the marriage cannot move forward stronger and happier than ever.

The truth is, you may never be able to give your spouse a "good reason" why it happened. There may not be a good reason. Perhaps it was just a stupid mistake. Perhaps you just wanted to do it and you indulged yourself.

You may not know yourself why it happened and you may be unwilling to attend personal counselling or talk therapy to figure it out. You may just want to repair the damage you have done and move forward without ever doing it again.

When it comes to infidelity, there is no standard explanation or approach. There is no "one size fits all."

You and your spouse may have to agree to work with what you have, with what you are willing to reveal, and make the choice to move forward in good faith.

Did Your Relationship Fall Prey To A "Partner Predator"?

It isn't always the unfaithful spouse who initiates the infidelity or opposite-sex friendship or who pursues the extramarital person. At times, an otherwise loving and devoted partner can fall prey to what I call "partner predators."

Partner predators find sport in seducing someone else's spouse or partner, and may go to great lengths to do so. They can be masters at exploiting another person's kindness, vanities, weaknesses or personality traits.

Take the classic case of a "lonely, heartbroken" man who seduces another man's wife by playing on her feminine sympathy. He might tell her how his ex-wife cheated on him and how much he wishes he could have met a woman like her instead.

He looks at her with those lovesick puppy-dog eyes until one day he steals a passionate but forbidden kiss. He knows it's wrong and he begs her forgiveness, but he can't help himself! She's just too beautiful and he cannot resist her any longer!

Before you know it, she's swept up in his passion and desire for her and the affair is underway. It's intoxicating. Of course, it's a bunch of bullshit. To him, it's all a game. He's managed to steal another man's wife, and that's quite the ego boost, isn't it?

Another classic example is the "damsel in distress" who seduces another woman's husband by playing on his masculine desire to feel needed.

She bats her eye-lashes at him and laughs at all his jokes, telling him what a wonderful man he is and how lucky his wife is to have him. Oh, if only she had such a strong, sexy man in her life!

She begins to "rely" on him for more things, until he begins to feel responsible for her. If she isn't asking him to look at her computer or help carry something heavy, she's asking him for his advice about her love life, planting seeds of intimacy.

And then one day as she's crying on his shoulder about how poorly yet another man has treated her, she manages – through her pretty tears – to place a soft, stolen kiss on his lips.

Before you know it, he's swept up in her need and love for him and the affair is underway. It's overwhelming. Of course, it's a bunch of bullshit. To her, it's all a game. She's managed to steal another woman's husband, and that's a real power trip, isn't it?

But what do partner predators do once they've "caught" their prey? That is, what happens when the betrayed spouse ends the marriage, thereby removing all obstacles to the affair?

Well, the partner predator then releases its prey. The thrill of the hunt is gone.

I sometimes compare partner predators to my cat Frosty. Frosty is a very spoiled animal. He has everything he could want; however, he loves the thrill of the hunt and even though his belly is always full, he will hunt mice in the back field and leave them on the doorstep just to prove that he's "still got it."

He never eats these mice. Sometimes he'll gnaw on their tail for a bit, but it's just for show. Once he's caught them, he doesn't want them anymore. He leaves them lying on the doorstep while he trots off, tail in the air, in search of another victim.

So why does he do it? Because it's in his nature. He's a cat. He's a predator.

The ugly truth is, some people are like this, too. Partner predators have nothing to lose in this game; however, they know that their "prey" has everything to lose. And that is part of the fun. That adds to the thrill of the hunt.

There is science to back this up. Research has demonstrated that some people are more attracted to members of the opposite-sex when they know the person is married or otherwise committed.

When told that a certain man or woman is "taken," these predator types experience a pleasurable rush of excitement caused by the brain chemical dopamine.

Dopamine – called the "pleasure and reward" hormone – is produced in increased amounts when a person is "in pursuit" of a potential romantic partner.

Partner predators can become addicted to this rush of pleasure and excitement, motivating them to "catch and release" prey over and over again.

I've seen this play out many times. Sometimes the partner predator will grow bored and leave its prey on the doorstep as soon as something sexual happens. Mission accomplished.

A more vicious species of partner predator will wait until its prey leaves his or her spouse and/or family – believing he or she has found true love – before being satisfied that the hunt is over. It then abandons its prey on the doorstep and sets off on a fresh hunt.

His or her baffled prey – the unfaithful spouse – is left to wonder what the hell happened. *"I thought you loved me?! I risked my marriage for you, and now you're just going to walk away?!"*

This discussion isn't meant to absolve you, as the person who broke your partner's trust, of your own behavior. **Even if you believe that you fell prey to a partner predator, you must acknowledge the pain you caused and be accountable for the actions you took.**

Rather, this discussion is meant to provide relevant and valuable insight into a scenario that I often see play out when it comes to infidelity. Good people can fall prey to bad people. It can be helpful for you and your partner to know that.

It can be particularly helpful for your spouse to know that you now see the extramarital partner for who he or she "really is." You see his or her "true colors" and are no longer under the illusion that he or she is a wonderful, good or desirable person.

Most betrayed partners want to feel vindicated in that way. They want to know that you are not secretly pining for the other person.   They want to know that they alone are in your heart.

From a defense standpoint, it's useful to know that partner predators are out there. If you can spot one from a distance, you can work together, as allies, to reinforce and guard the fortress around your marriage and/or family unit.

I've tried to give Frosty's prey that kind of heads-up. He now wears a flashing neon collar with a bell so that hopefully his prey can see and hear him coming.

Even in the best of marriages and with the strongest of fortresses, partner predators can come sniffing around from time to time. You never when or how they'll strike or which spouse might be the prey. But if you are wise to their "wolf in sheep's clothing" ways, you can chase them away before they go in for the kill.

Was Your Relationship Sabotaged By A "Spouse Scavenger"?

If you'll indulge another animal metaphor, I'd like to briefly tell you about the shady habits of the common cuckoo bird. The common cuckoo is what's called a "brood parasite."

Instead of going through the trouble of building its own nest, the cuckoo waits – watching from a distance – as another pair of birds builds a nest together and the female lays her eggs in it.

Then, when this pair of birds isn't looking, the cuckoo swoops down into their nest, kicks out one of their eggs, and lays its own egg in their nest. It sabotages, for its own benefit, what the mating pair has already created.

I'm not beating up on the cuckoo bird, here. I wouldn't question the wisdom of Mother Nature. But it is a fairly distasteful tactic, isn't it?

Unfortunately, it sometimes happens that a similar scene plays out within relationships. There are some people who are very drawn to a man or woman who is already taken. Partner predators fall into this category.

So do what I call "spouse scavengers." These people are attracted to those in committed relationships and, like partner predators, can be very manipulative and aggressive when going after what they want.

Yet unlike partner predators – who dispose of their prey once caught – spouse scavengers want to keep what they have found. They want to swoop in and replace the more established spouse/mate.

When I was single, my girlfriends and I used to talk about the qualities we found most attractive in men. Many of us were attracted to the "marrying" type of man. The type of man who was devoted to his wife and family.

Why? Because that type of man has already demonstrated his willingness to commit.

The better husband he is to his wife, the better father he is to his own kids, the more we want him to be our husband and the father to our kids. He's a good bet. He displays the qualities we are looking for. I guess it's kind of instinctual.

Unfortunately, some women do more than just talk about their attraction to committed men. Let me walk you through an example.

In my part of the world, oil and gas is the predominant industry and I work with many "oil patch couples."

In a typical arrangement, a husband might be gone for weeks at a time, travelling to various towns and job sites, as his wife stays home to manage the house, the kids and maybe work full or part-time.

Unfortunately, these husbands often catch the eye of single or divorced women who are attracted to the high-income of oil men and the security that comes with it.

One particular case comes to my mind. The husband was regularly sent to work in a small town in the northern part of the province, often spending three weeks out of every month there, while his wife held down the fort at home, many miles away in the southern part of the province.

They had two kids, a good marriage and did the best they could to make the situation work.

This particular small town had only one pub. It was the gathering place for many oil workers – and the local women who wanted to snag one.

One of these women, who was also a single mom, was known to flirt with almost every oil man she came across; however, when she met this particular husband, she was particularly smitten.

He was an established supervisor, had a company truck and was the only man on his crew that was married and proud of it. The other guys were either single or divorced, and made it very clear that marriage wasn't on their agenda anytime soon.

The extramarital relationship between them started off slowly. The woman pretended to be interested in a single guy on the husband's crew, which gave her an excuse to befriend him.

She found out his phone number and began to text him, sometimes innocently and sometimes more intimately. She would corner him when he came into the pub alone, and cry on his shoulder about how mean her ex-boyfriend was and how she was in the middle of a battle with him over child-support payments.

One night after a few too many drinks – and assuring him that she had her "tubes tied" and could not get pregnant – she made her big move and they had sex.

Full of remorse and feelings of self-disgust, the husband ended it the next morning. He had himself tested for sexually-transmitted disease and asked his employer to send him to a different job site in the future.

But the deed was done – she was pregnant. She tried calling and texting to tell him, but he had blocked her phone number. Finally, she called his employer and, impersonating his wife, managed to get through to him on a different job site.

He was shattered. Not only did he have to tell his wife about the extramarital relationship and the breach in trust, he had to tell her about the baby.

It was a brutal revelation; however, he had done everything right in the wake of the infidelity, and those gestures reassured his wife that he was truly remorseful. She decided to stay and work on rebuilding their relationship.

This couple believed that the other woman had deliberately gotten pregnant, most likely so that she could collect the significant child-support payments from the husband.

But the other woman, who already had a four-year-old daughter and another child on the way – didn't just want a monthly check. She wanted the whole package.

She knew he had a big house, two or three vehicles, a boat, a summer cottage at the lake and a nanny for the children. He had the resources to afford the type of lifestyle that she could only dream about. He was her ticket to a fuller, richer "insta-life."

More importantly, he had already demonstrated his willingness to get married, father children and work hard for his wife and family – and that was *exactly* what she wanted and needed in a man.

Her goal was for the husband to divorce his wife and marry her. Her plan was to move into his house as his new wife and step-parent his previous children while they raised their new child together as one big happy blended family.

And she did everything she could to sabotage the now fragile relationship between him and his wife.

She did everything she could to shake their nest badly enough that the wife would finally give up and fly away, leaving her to move in.

Although the husband and his wife managed to work through this very serious case of infidelity and stay together, it took a very long time – and eventually a restraining order – for the other woman to abandon her efforts to "supplant" the man's wife.

Is that cuckoo behavior? Maybe. Or maybe in this case, the other woman's efforts were driven as much by economic need and survival as anything else. Regardless, this example does illustrate how the spouse scavenger operates.

While I have in the past typically seen this behavior more on the part of women than men, that is changing.

The playing field appears to be leveling out, especially as more single men complain they are having trouble finding "wife material" in the hook-up culture that characterizes today's dating landscape.

I've heard many single men say they feel increasingly drawn toward the stability, lifestyle choices and maternal nature of married women, including those who already have children.

Their assumption is that these married women are somehow more desirable or higher-quality because they've already been "snapped up" by other men. *"If he wanted her that badly, then she must be a real catch!"*

They believe that these women will be able to provide the storybook family life they are looking for, as well as being ideal mothers for their children.

And they believe that, if they play their cards right, they can seduce these women away from their current husbands and family units to set-up their own insta-family arrangement with them.

Again, the scenario I've presented here and this discussion isn't meant to pardon your behavior. It may having absolutely nothing to do with your situation.

It is only meant to provide relevant insight into the complicated dynamics and various agendas that are at play in some cases of infidelity.

Partner predators and spouse scavengers are out there and they can wreak havoc on otherwise stable marriages.

If you believe this personality type factored into your infidelity, it is fine to share this insight with your spouse; however, you must never try to blame the other person for what you have done.

Nonetheless, the more you can understand why your marital fortress suffered this breach in trust, and the more you can recognize the saboteur tactics used by the person who managed to break through, the more you and your spouse can work as allies to repair that breach and prevent it from happening again.

Questions To Ask Yourself:
How To Avoid Saying "I Don't Know"

No doubt your spouse is full of questions right now. The biggest question may be, "Why did you do it?"

We've discussed several common reasons why, from stupid mistakes and personal technology to pre-existing problems and partner predators; however, you will still want to put your own unique situation under the microscope and examine your own reasons.

Preparation is always a good thing. Before you and your spouse have a heart-to-heart discussion about why the affair, indiscretion, or opposite-sex friendship happened, you would be wise to ask yourself some probing questions first.

Why should you do this? To avoid having to say the words, "I don't know" to your spouse when he or she asks you a question about why you did it, whether you were unhappy in the marriage, how the other person made you feel and so on.

Nothing is more frustrating to a betrayed spouse than asking his or her partner, *"Why did you do it? Were you in some way unhappy with the marriage? Were you unhappy with me?"* and getting a blank-faced *"I don't know"* as a response.

It is impossible to collaborate with a person who will not participate in the process. Unless you can provide your spouse with some level of self-awareness and understanding, it is unlikely that he or she will believe you are truly remorseful or trust you again.

After reading some of the previous reasons, you may have great insight into your situation. Or you may still have little insight. Regardless, the following questions may help steer you toward some honest self-reflection and organize your thoughts.

Keep in mind: While some of these questions concern past complaints you may have had about your spouse, marriage or lifestyle, the purpose is not to pass blame onto your spouse. You must at all times be fully accountable for your own actions.

Questions of this nature are meant to deepen insight in an effort to move forward in a positive way, not point fingers.

Read through the following questions. Some may be very relevant, while others not at all.

• What complaints have I expressed about my spouse in the past? (i.e. critical, defensive, negative, not supportive, over-spends, not affectionate or sexually attentive, doesn't show appreciation, lazy, an indifferent parent, always on the computer or phone, etc.)

- What past complaints have I expressed about our marriage or our lifestyle? (i.e. debt load, too busy, disorganized or messy household, skewed priorities, too much technology in the home, opposite-sex friendships, unhealthy diet or lack of exercise, child-centered marriage, no couple time, etc.)

- What appealed to me about the other person? Did I feel needed or desired by the other person? Did I feel admired, appreciated or adored by the other person?

- What appealed to me about the situation? Was the situation exciting, liberating, fun or stress-free? Did it bring a "thrill" to the routine of my day?

- What role did personal technology (i.e. smartphones, computers, social media, etc.) play in all of this? How did my use of personal technology influence my behavior and choices?

- What has been going on in my life lately? Have I been struggling with any personal or professional issues?

- What are my greatest fears? (i.e. getting older, being unsuccessful at work, etc.) Did these fears factor into my actions?

- What was my self-perception before the affair, indiscretion or opposite-sex friendship? That is, how did I see or think about myself before I started to see the other person?

- What was my self-perception during the affair, indiscretion or opposite-sex friendship? That is, how did I feel about myself while I was seeing the other person?

In addition to knowing that you have some level of insight into why the infidelity happened and what drew you to the other person, your spouse will want to know that you understand:

a) how your attitude and behavior contributed to any pre-existing problems in the marriage, and

b) how your actions have impacted your spouse and/or your family unit.

You may be very aware of these things, or you may be largely unaware of them. Regardless, the following questions may help steer you toward a better understanding so that your spouse sees your humility and feels understood and validated.

Again, some of these questions may be very relevant, while others not at all. One thing is for sure, though – some may be hard to read and even harder to answer. Answering them honestly will require great humility and a willingness to be critical of yourself.

Keep in mind the purpose of these questions isn't to berate you or make you feel worse than you already do about your actions.

Rather, the purpose of these questions is for you to gain insight into how your behavior impacted your spouse, and to show your spouse that you have done so. Before your spouse can forgive you and move forward, he or she needs to know that you "get it."

Remember your goal: To have a purposeful heart-to-heart conversation with your spouse, one that is about understanding, not blame. The more honest and comprehensive you can make these conversations, the fewer of them you will have to engage in.

- What complaints have I expressed to my spouse about him/her? Might my spouse be feeling unduly criticized, unloved or unappreciated? How might my complaints have made my spouse feel about himself/herself?

- What complaints have I expressed to my spouse about our marriage or lifestyle? Might my spouse be feeling like I am unhappy with the life we've built together?

- Have I been putting effort into our emotional intimacy? Might my spouse be feeling unimportant, unloved or not prioritized?

- Have I been putting effort into our sexual intimacy? Might my spouse be feeling sexually rejected or unloved?

- Have I been making my spouse feel appreciated?

- Have I been making my spouse feel desired?

- What is the "vibe" in our marriage and home? Does our home have a happy, supportive, easygoing, good-humored vibe? Or does it have a negative, critical and cold vibe?

- Have I been there for my children? Do I set aside time to spend with them? Am I an involved, interested and loving parent?

- Did I prioritize being or communicating with the other person over being with my children? What message does that send to my children? What might my children be thinking about me?

- Have I been showing friendship to my spouse?

- What has been going on in my spouse's life lately? Has my spouse been struggling with any personal challenges or professional issues?

- How did I contribute to the current state of our marriage? How have I hurt my spouse or let him or her down?

- Do I prioritize the needs of my spouse and/or children?

- How did I feel when I was lying to my spouse?

- When my spouse approached me with questions or concerns about my behavior, how did I react? Did I try to make my spouse feel like he or she was just being insecure? How must that have made my spouse feel?

- Did I defend the other person to my spouse? That is, did I stick up for the other person when my spouse said something about him or her? How must that have made my spouse feel?

- How do I think living in a state of suspicion affected my spouse? How did it affect my spouse's ability to parent our children or perform domestic or work duties?

- Might my spouse be comparing himself or herself to the other person? Did I ever compare my spouse to the other person? How must that make my spouse feel about himself or herself?

- How much time away from the home did I devote to being with or communicating with the other person? Did this force my spouse to take on more responsibilities with the children?

- How might my spouse have felt when I left the room to text or call the other person in private?

- What do I think my partner felt when he or she discovered the affair or opposite-sex friendship?

- What perception might my spouse have of me and my value as a spouse?

- How did I tend to interact with my spouse while I was seeing the other person?

- If I had a time machine and could go back, what would I do differently?

Questions To Ask Your Spouse

There comes a time when spouses who are struggling with broken trust will be ready to have a sincere "heart-to-heart" conversation about why it happened and how to rebuild trust.

This conversation isn't about blaming or hurting each other. It's about understanding why the marriage fell victim to an affair, indiscretion or inappropriate friendship, so that it can be stronger and happier moving forward.

The best heart-to-heart conversations happen naturally and fluidly. Some couples are able to have a conversation that flows freely yet purposefully. They don't need a map to get where they need to go.

Other couples need a little direction. It may be that they struggle with expressing themselves verbally or that they have no idea how to even start talking about the infidelity.

Generally, I'm not a fan of "scripted" relationship questions. Too often they come across as forced, artificial and insincere, and that can undermine the authenticity and natural flow of a true heart-to-heart conversation.

That being said, scripted questions can provide a map that can take spouses where they need to go, especially if those spouses don't know how to begin the conversation or don't communicate well verbally.

After all, it's certainly better to move forward with a map than to stay in one place spinning your wheels.

I've included some questions that can be used as "talking points." Their purpose is to open and facilitate a dialogue.

Don't worry about sticking to the map. If you ask a question and the answer takes the conversation elsewhere, go with it. The sooner you and your spouse can find your own way to talk about your problems and your marriage, the better.

As always, some of these questions will be relevant to your situation and helpful, others not at all. I have provided many questions here; however, I wouldn't tackle too many at once. Take it slow and steady.

Finally, keep in mind that it isn't always necessary (or possible) to find the answer to some questions. Sometimes, asking the question is enough because it makes a spouse feel heard and validated.

Discussing these questions can show that you acknowledge your part, that you want to understand why the breach in trust happened, and that you want to ensure it doesn't happen again.

- In what ways were you unhappy with me before the infidelity/indiscretion began?

- In what ways were you unhappy with our marriage, family life or lifestyle before the infidelity/indiscretion began?

- Did you / do you feel appreciated in our marriage?

- Did you / do you feel heard and understood by me?

- Did you/ do you feel like you are a priority to me?

- Did you / do you feel supported in our marriage?

- Do you think we have a child-centered marriage?

- How do you feel about being a parent? What did you/ do you find challenging about it? Do you think that we co-parent well?

- Do you think I am a good parent? How might I be better?

- Do you think we've had good emotional intimacy in our marriage? If not, what did you feel was missing?

- Do you think we've had good sexual intimacy in our marriage? If not, what did you feel was missing?

- What do you worry about? (i.e. finances and debt, getting older, health issues, the kids, your aging parents, etc.)

- Were you / are you struggling with any stressors or anxiety? If so, were you and I working together to relieve them?

- Before the infidelity/indiscretion, how did you see and feel about yourself? That is, what was your self-perception?

- How do you see and feel about yourself now? That is, what effect has all of this had on your self-perception?

- What role do you think technology (i.e. smartphones, texting, computers, social media, etc.) has played in all of this?

- How did you feel when I would text the other person in secret or leave the room to call him or her?

- How did you feel when I locked my phone or computer and wouldn't let you look at it?

- Did you ever compare yourself to the other person?

- Did you ever feel like you had to compete with the other person?

- Did you ever feel that I defended the other person or took his / her side instead of yours?

- Did I ever pressure you to "get over it"? How did that make you feel?

- Did I ever try to convince you that you were paranoid or controlling because of your suspicions? How did that make you feel about the situation and about me?

- What effects do you think my actions have had our on children?

- Did my actions put extra demands on you at home or with the kids?

- How do you think I contributed to the current state of our marriage? How have I hurt you or let you down?

- How do you think you contributed to the current state of our marriage? How have you hurt me or let me down?

- What do you think is preventing us from rebuilding trust?

- What have I been doing that has been helping you feel more trusting toward me and more positive?

- What could I do that would make you feel more trusting toward me or more positive?

- What do you think might still be standing in the way of our efforts to make our marriage stronger and happier?

- If you could go back, what would you do differently?

- Do you feel that you and I go through life as allies? If not, how can we start to do that?

- How can you and I work together to build a fortress around our marriage and family?

Approach these questions with empathy and, as importantly, with a curious spirit. The point is not to debate or disagree with your spouse, or to defend your actions. The point is to acknowledge the impact that your extramarital relationship had on your spouse, and to understand why it happened.

That kind of understanding is important. Once you know where the weakness in your relationship was or is, you can do what's necessary to repair and strengthen it.

Alternatives To "Talking About It"

I'm often asked by spouses whether it's okay to write their partner a letter instead of "talking about it." My answer is Yes, providing that the letter is meant to complement communication and understanding, not just act as substitute for more intimate face-to-face forms of communication.

Letter writing can be useful when a person is dealing with a spouse who is particularly emotional or defensive, and who isn't otherwise receptive to hearing his or her partner out.

Take the case of a husband who has recently ended a sexual affair with a co-worker. His wife is demanding that he quit his job and look for a different one.

Whenever the husband tries to express his concerns about this – he knows he won't find a good-paying job in the current market – his wife storms of out the room, accusing him of wanting to continue the affair.

In a situation like this, writing a letter is better than just falling into the same predictable pattern of conflict, defensiveness and anger.

It may be more productive for the husband to write a letter that expresses his fear about their financial situation if he quits his job, and his concern that financial strain will only add to the problems they are dealing with.

In the letter, he can go on to express his commitment to his wife and outline any proactive steps he has taken to limit contact with the other person. These are things he doesn't get to say when she cuts him off and storms out of the room.

Letter writing can also be helpful for spouses who find it challenging to express themselves verbally, and who need extra time to think through their thoughts and statements.

Some people are very good at putting their foot in their mouth. Writing a letter can help them organize their ideas and write them down in a respectful, coherent way.

For people who are reluctant or embarrassed to share their feelings, letter writing can help them explore and express their emotions without feeling like they're in the spotlight or that they might reveal something they aren't ready to share.

If you choose to write your spouse a letter, be sure to self-check your writing for tone, negativity, accusation, blame and assumption. People always read between the lines, so take care.

Remember that the goal of the letter is to express yourself with honesty and respect, and to encourage your spouse to do likewise. The goal is to open or enhance a dialogue.

The goal of the letter is not to write down every nasty thought you have about your spouse simply because he or she is not there to stop you.

A quick word here about texting. I strongly advise against using text messages as a way to talk about anything, never mind something as emotional and potentially explosive as infidelity.

Text messages are inherently open to misinterpretation. And whenever a person who reads a text message misinterprets it, he or she always does so in the worst way possible.

A word that is mistakenly sent in ALL CAPS comes across as a loud, angry yell. A message that ends without a heart emoticon comes across as abrupt and insensitive. It just isn't worth the risk.

An alternative to letter-writing, one that people don't think of as much, is voice-recording a message that you can send to your spouse or that spouses can exchange with each other.

Voice recordings can be done on almost any smartphone and have all the advantages of letter writing. They let a spouse speak in a relaxed tone, without being interrupted by the other spouse or facing the other spouse's defensiveness.

Yet they also have an advantage over letter writing because they are able to convey emotion in a more sincere and accurate way. Tone of voice can limit the guesswork or assumption that sometimes happens when someone reads a written letter.

A voice recording can also act as a take-anywhere message of reassurance. Whenever a spouse is feeling fearful about the relationship or having flashbacks of anger or suspicion, he or she can simply hit playback on a smartphone and hear his or her spouse's reassuring voice speak words of love, devotion and so on.

So as you can see, there are viable alternatives to "talking about it," or at least to talking it to death.

There have to be. People are all different and couples have their own strengths and weaknesses. You have to work with what you have.

Yet many couples who are trying to rebuild trust mistakenly assume that their only choice for professional help is counselling or talk therapy.

Due to the prevalence of talk therapy in our culture, there is certainly the assertion that "talking about it" is the only way to get over it. The more you talk about it, the better.

This idea persists even though talk therapy has a poor success rate in terms of helping couples rebuild their marriages.

It persists even though men in particular are often exceedingly uncomfortable with it. It persists even though many couples say they fight in the car on the drive home from the talk-therapist or counselor's office.

Indeed, a good portion of my clientele has always been comprised of "counselling drop-outs." These are folks who have grown frustrated with the slow, ongoing nature of counselling and of "talking it to death" every week, always digging up that dead cat and then burying it again.

They're sick of wallowing in the mistake and in the negative emotions and memories that surround it. They're sick of reliving it, pointing fingers and complaining about each other.

Let me be clear: I completely agree that spouses must talk about their problems, feelings, fears, hopes and so on. There is no doubt that talking about the infidelity or indiscretion is necessary for spouses to feel heard and understood, and to agree on changes that must be made if the marriage is to survive and thrive.

But talking is not the only form of communicating a thought or emotion. Sometimes there are more authentic and appropriate ways, especially when our throats are hoarse from talking.

Sometimes a loving embrace can say *"I adore you, I cherish you"* far more intimately than words could.

Sometimes a gentle squeeze of hand or a soft kiss on the cheek can say *"I am sorry"* in a much more sincere way that words could.

Sometimes a warm smile can say *"I know what you're thinking, but I love you and everything will be okay"* in a more heartfelt and reassuring way than words ever could.

Actions Speak Louder Than Words

Many betrayed spouses know all too well that talk is cheap. They may have asked their spouse "Are you cheating on me?" a hundred times, and a hundred times heard him or her say, "No, I would never cheat on you!" Words don't always speak the truth.

In the end, actions may be more reliable. In fact, I have a little saying that I often tell my clients: If the words and the actions don't match, believe the actions.

For example, let's say a couple is trying to recover after the wife's emotional affair. The husband asks her, "Did you text him today?" The wife says, "No," but then refuses to let her husband look at her phone which, incidentally, is password protected.

This doesn't exactly convey a sense of trustworthiness, does it? Actions sometimes speak louder than words.

Now let's say the wife leaves her cell phone – unlocked and fully accessible to her husband – on the kitchen counter at all times. Whenever he wants, he can pick it up and scroll through the messages.

In this case, the husband may not even ask if she has texted the other man. Her actions make the question unnecessary.   Her actions speak volumes about her honesty and intent.

Spouses, even those in conflict, usually know each other pretty well. They know what makes each other happy, sad, reassured, fearful. They know what actions they can take to make each other's days easier and nights more enjoyable.

If they are motivated, they can recall their spouse's complaints and, by putting some thought into it, come up with ways to address those complaints for the greater good of the marriage.

Consider this example. A husband has been complaining that he doesn't feel appreciated by his wife. She says, "Well, tell me what I can do to make you feel appreciated?"

He answers, "I don't know...maybe get the kids to take better care of their electronics so that I don't feel like I'm working for nothing."

The next day, the kids are fooling around when they break a costly video-game controller. The wife chastises the kids and says, "Your dad wants you to take better care of your things!"

The husband storms out of the room. The wife follows him and says, "Why are you pissed off? I did what you said!"

The husband throws up his arms. "You didn't do anything! You just managed to make me look like the bad guy yet again."

How different would this have played out if, once the wife knew the husband's complaint – feeling unappreciated by her and their children – she put some thought into more sincere ways to make him feel appreciated.

For example, she might have met her husband at the door after work and encouraged her children to do the same saying, "Let's welcome dad home. He's worked hard all day."

I'm willing to bet that this simple act of thoughtfulness and appreciation would mean more to this husband than a video-game controller.

These are simple examples, but they illustrate an important point. **Spouses who are trying to rebuild trust need to focus on their actions. Our actions can convey our thoughts, feelings and priorities in some very powerful ways.**

Ask yourself these simple questions: When were we the happiest as a couple? When did my spouse seem to be the most in love with me?

These questions are a fantastic starting point. It may be that you and your spouse were the happiest when you used to surprise each other with week-end getaways. Try to do that again.

Even if your circumstances have changed – let's say you have kids or don't have as much disposable income – you can still reproduce the freedom of the experience to some extent, even if it's just by leaving the kids at grandma's for the night and having a dinner-and-movie night at home.

It may be that, once you start thinking about it, you realize your spouse seemed most in love with you when you encouraged him or her spend time with friends or engage in a favorite hobby.

You may remember that your spouse seemed happiest and treated you the best when you had more outside interests and the two of you weren't spending every minute together.

You may begin to compare the way you speak to and interact with your spouse now with the way you used to speak to and interact with your spouse, and in the process you may realize that your voice tone has become critical and your behavior has become cold and indifferent.

And as you do this, your spouse notices the change. He or she notices your efforts to spend child-free nights together, to give him or her more social time with good friends, and to reassure him or her about your commitment to the relationship in sweet ways.

Your spouse notices the softer tones in your voice and the way you reach out to give him or her a gentle caress on the shoulder or a kiss on the cheek.

And as your spouse delights in these efforts and changes, he or she is motivated to make similar efforts and changes for you. Loving behavior sparks loving behavior. Kind words spark kind words. Effort and change spark effort and change.

Sex & Love:
Two Sides Of The Same Coin

Happy couples know an important truth about marriage: emotional and sexual intimacy are two sides of the same coin. This coin must always remain spinning so that the value of both sides can be seen.

If one side is always up while the other is turned down, or if one side is assumed to have more value than the other side, problems are going to happen. There's no way around it.

This is often seen as the classic "love vs. sex" debate; however, emotional intimacy isn't just about feeling loved.

It's also about feeling appreciated, adored, respected, desired and validated. It's about being recognized for who you are. Emotional intimacy is enhanced by talking, touching, laughing, supporting and prioritizing each other.

It is strengthened by working "as a team" in all things, including resolving conflict.

Sexual intimacy – believe it or not – is about many of the same things.

Why? Because a person who does not feel loved, appreciated, desired and so on by his or her spouse is unlikely to feel the full spectrum of pleasure that true sexual intimacy provides.

Of course, spouses may gravitate toward one side or the other. A husband may feel more loving toward his wife, and be willing to show her more non-sexual affection, when she is having frequent and enjoyable sex with him.

At the same time, his wife may feel more sexually attracted to him, and be willing to engage in more frequent and enjoyable sex, when he is showing her more non-sexual affection.

You can see how that creates a vicious circle, right? It also creates a "you go first" mentality where spouses basically wait each other out in what can best be described as a pissing contest:

"I'm not going to have sex with you until I feel more loved and supported outside the bedroom."

vs.

"Why should I help you if you won't even have sex with me? My needs are important too, you know."

It's a deadlock. But it's a deadlock that's easy enough to break if one partner chooses to prioritize his or her spouse's needs, thereby sending the message that re-establishing intimacy is more important than getting the other person to "give in."

A caveat here: I'm not suggesting that a spouse have sex with a partner who isn't acting in a loving or respectful way. Doing so will only create more problems.

I am, however, suggesting that showing your spouse that you care about his or her needs can motivate that partner to care about your needs.

Many spouses who are struggling with some form of infidelity or indiscretion will say they didn't feel their emotional and/or sexual needs for intimacy were being met in the marriage.

Meeting these needs isn't just necessary to rebuild trust and save a marriage. It is also necessary to prevent breaches of trust from happening again.

"When Should We Sleep Together Again?"

While there's no "right" answer to this question, here is my general guideline: When both spouses understand that emotional and sexual intimacy are two sides of the same coin, and when both spouses are committed to meeting each other's needs for them, then it's probably okay to start sleeping together again.

Don't get me wrong – other factors may need to be present as well, such as a clean bill of sexual health, an assurance that the extramarital relationship has ended, a genuine display of remorse or a few productive heart-to-heart conversations.

Ultimately, it should be up to the spouse whose trust was broken to decide whether he or she is ready to have sex with his or her spouse again. A betrayed spouse should never feel pressured.

"I Thought We Were Making Progress?"
How To Help Your Spouse Cope With Flashbacks

Earlier in this part of the book I touched on triggers. These are the emotions – fear, sadness, a sense of betrayal, insecurity, and many others – that can cause a person to lash out in any number of ways.

Memories and thought processes can trigger emotional outbursts, too.

There will be times when your spouse is unexpectedly flooded with memories, thoughts and emotions about some very unpleasant things.

This can happen even if much time has passed, and even if the two of you have made real progress in terms of rebuilding trust and strengthening your marriage.

It is perfectly normal for a spouse whose trust has been broken to experience mental and emotional flashbacks, even very intense ones; however, it can be very disheartening for a couple, especially if they have begun to think that the worst is behind them.

A betrayed spouse may say, "I'll never get over this," while the unfaithful spouse may say, "I thought you were over this?" When this happens, many couples begin to argue and talk about the infidelity or indiscretion as if it had just happened.

To avoid falling into this "talking it to death" trap, I often recommend that the spouse whose trust has been broken recognize his or her triggers and have a "signal" that he or she can send the other spouse when bad memories, feelings or flashbacks strike.

When the other spouse sees that signal, he or she reacts with reassurance, support, love and so on. This is a great way for a couple to act as a team.

For example, take the case of a stay-at-home mom and wife whose husband had a sexual affair a year ago. They have worked hard to rebuild trust and improve their marriage; however, every now and then, the wife's mind begins to wander.

This tends to happen after she has put her baby daughter down for her morning nap. The house is quiet and she has time to sit at the kitchen table alone and think...and to think back.

And that's exactly what she does. She thinks back to every gory detail, every lie and deception, every hurt and heartache. By the time her husband gets home after work, she is in angry tears and the fight is on. Again.

In this case, the wife tends to be triggered by silence and idleness. If she were more aware of that, she would be able to take steps to avoid being triggered (or at least to avoid being triggered as often).

She might choose to play music or call a friend during that time. She might choose to exercise or to work on a project.

In addition, she could "signal" her spouse for support by sending a short text message that lets him know she needs some kind of reassurance from him.

This signal might be something that they have agreed upon together, such as the year they were married.

When the husband receives a text from her that reads "2012," he knows that he needs to give her a quick call or reassuring text to show his support.

These signals can happen in person, too. Let's say a couple is enjoying a social event when the husband sees a man who looks disconcertingly like the man his wife had an affair with.

Instead of letting his thoughts and emotions get away from him like a runaway train, he signals his wife – perhaps by rubbing his hands together – that he needs her support.

When she sees this, she makes an extra effort to be affectionate and loving to him.

When it comes to rebuilding trust after an affair or indiscretion, long-term thinking is essential. You must be in it for the long haul. You must know that it will sometimes seem like you're taking two steps forward and one step back.

Yet by:

a) helping your spouse recognize his or her triggers

b) helping your spouse brainstorm ways to manage those triggers, and

c) responding quickly and sincerely to your spouse's signals for support or reassurance

….you can ensure that the steps forward get bigger every day. Remember: Empathy. Humility. Patience.

How To Prevent It From Happening Again

Many couples successfully rebuild their marriages after trust has been broken. In fact, some couples even say they are better off because of it all.

The affair, indiscretion or inappropriate opposite-sex friendship forced them to face the weak spots in their marriage. It forced them to work together to repair and then strengthen them.

For some couples, this crisis marked the first time they worked as allies to do anything positive. I hope that will be your experience, and that this book can help you make it happen.

I encourage you to flip through the pages of this book from time to time, and especially during those times you feel a strain on your marriage. Doing so can remind you of some simple yet powerful strategies that can keep your marital alliance strong.

I will leave you with ten snapshot strategies that encompass some of the big-picture ideas put forth in this book. These are concepts that can affair-proof and divorce-proof a marriage.

By incorporating these strategies into your relationship on a daily basis, you will be laying the foundation for a marriage and home that is built on very strong ground indeed.

1. **Listen to your spouse's complaints or concerns.** It is foolish, short-sighted and selfish to shrug off a partner's complaints, whether they are about housework, money, a lack of affection, in-laws or texting.

   It is even worse to become ignorant or defensive when your partner tries to express the reasons for his or her unhappiness. You don't need to agree with what he or she is saying; however, you do need to listen, care and do something to improve the situation.

   Keep your ears open: when you hear your partner express something he or she is unhappy with in the marriage or home, stop what you're doing and listen. Instead of just arguing, show your spouse that you care about his or her happiness and are willing to work together.

2. **Express your own complaints or concerns.** Instead of bottling up your feelings and expecting your spouse to read your mind, be open about whatever it is that is bothering you. Just be sure that you always do this in a way that is productive and respectful of your partner's feelings and perspective.

   If the issue is an emotional or potentially volatile one, set the conversation up for success by choosing a good time to talk and by setting a positive mood.

3. **Build a fortress around your marriage.** Strong marriages have a wall of privacy around them. This wall keeps in feelings of love, devotion, respect, friendship and family solidarity. It shields the marriage from the view of outsiders while allowing for total transparency inside, between spouses (i.e. shared passwords on phones and computers).

   This wall also keeps certain things out, including destructive emotions or assumptions, negative behaviors, and people would could potentially chip away at a couple's bond (i.e. opposite-sex friends and intruding in-laws).

4. **Put technology in its place.** Translation: Put down the damn phone and talk to your spouse and kids! Log out of social media and have a movie night with your family. Stop texting friends or pointlessly surfing the Internet and start connecting with the people that matter in your life.

Fight the impulse to check your phone for messages or email every five minutes. Put your phone in a drawer at night and engage in some pillow-talk with your sweetheart instead.

5. **Speak to and interact with your spouse like he or she is someone you love.** Speak with love – not criticism, contempt or defensiveness – in your voice tone. Use positive body language. Remember your manners. Greet your spouse at the door with a kiss. Praise your spouse in front of your children.

   Offer a smile instead of a frown, a flirtatious wink instead of a scowl. Caress your partner's shoulder as you walk by. Be someone that your spouse wants to come home to. There are a hundred ways you can show your spouse, every day, that you are grateful to have him or her in your life.

6. **Nourish emotional intimacy.** Stay tuned-in to what is happening in your spouse's life. Is he or she going through a hard time at work? Is he or she trying to eat healthier? Whatever it is, use it as an opportunity to show your spouse that a) you actually notice what is going on in his or her life and b) you truly care and are there to offer encouragement and support.

   Remind yourself often that your spouse isn't just a fixture in your home – he or she is a human being with his or her own feelings, fears, hopes and struggles. Shower your spouse with respect, appreciation, adoration, non-sexual affection, true friendship and love.

7. **Don't let sex fall off the radar.** Sex is a big part of marriage. In fact, regular sexual access to a person they love is a prevailing reason that people get married. Order-in supper more often, put the kids to bed earlier, chew on a handful of chocolate-covered coffee beans before bed — do whatever it takes to keep some energy for sex.

   As importantly, be sure that your sex life remains fun and pleasurable. Let your spouse know that you desire him or her by showing sexual enthusiasm and taking the initiative to "spice it up" once in a while with sex toys, erotica, etc.

8. **Put your spouse's needs and happiness ahead of your own.** This doesn't mean that your needs or happiness come second. The needs and happiness of both spouses in a marriage are equal; however, by putting your spouse ahead of yourself, you set the tone for a marriage where both spouses are "competing" to meet each other's needs and make each other happy. Now *that's* a dream marriage.

9. **Create a happy household vibe.** Most of us have walked into a house where you feel like you could cut the tension with a knife. Those who live there are growly, argumentative and seem to actively dislike one another. Most of us have walked into a different type of house too, the type where warmth and happiness envelopes you as soon as you pass through the door. Those who live there seem to genuinely enjoy each other's company. The vibe is easygoing, friendly and relaxed.

Strive for the latter household! Create a happy vibe in your home where your spouse and your children co-exist in love, friendship and good-humor. Work as allies with your spouse and/or kids to share household duties and domestic chores, always showing your appreciation for their solidarity and support.

10. **Be a whole person.** It's a fact of married life: happy spouses make happy marriages.

A person who is at peace with his or her life and who strives to exhibit positive personality traits (i.e. open-mindedness, an easygoing nature, good humor, emotional control, reliability, humility, etc.) is far more likely to be a loving and loved spouse than someone who doesn't have these qualities.

Strive to be the best, happiest person you can be outside of your marriage and you will find that your marriage reflects who you are.

Closing Issues

To Be Read By Both Spouses

Resisting Temptation

Once you begin to understand why the breach of trust happened in your marriage, and after you've taken steps to rebuild trust and revive your relationship, you will want to work together to prevent it from happening again.

The ten snapshot strategies included in the "How to Prevent it From Happening Again" sections at the end of Part I and Part II can help you do this by building a solid foundation of good communication, positive interactions and intimacy-enhancing marital habits.

Yet there's one more thing I'd like to mention here: specifically, the role of temptation.

Regardless of the reason for the broken trust – whether it was a deeper marital issue or pure boredom – all wayward spouses have something in common: they gave in, to some extent, to temptation.

And that's something all of us can identify with. We've all given in to temptation of one kind or another. A cigarette. A piece of cheesecake. A glass of wine or bottle of beer. An impulse purchase. A mean or thoughtless action or statement.

Of course, sexual temptation is the most intense form of temptation a human being can experience. It creates unparalleled feelings of excitement and lust, and it can compel even a very loving and committed partner to cross a line.

I'm not excusing the behavior by any means. Nor am I saying that monogamy is impossible.

Quite the opposite, in fact. Countless couples have made it work. Armed with a) insight, b) commitment to your marriage, and c) practical strategies to resist temptation, you can make it work, too.

First, insight. A partner who has given in to temptation must have insight into their own body's physiological responses when faced with erotic temptation.

He or she must recognize how powerful those feelings of sexual arousal are, so that he or she doesn't mistakenly assume that those feelings must be acted upon, that they mean something is "missing" from the marriage, or that they indicate feelings of "true love" for the tempter. None of those things may be true.

Because this guide isn't focused on the particulars of sexual arousal, I encourage couples to do some basic research into this area so that they can gain a greater understanding of what is happening to them – physically, chemically, mentally and emotionally – when they are presented with an extramarital sexual temptation.

Forewarned is forearmed. Be conscious of the way your body and mind respond to erotic stimuli – that will give you a greater sense of awareness and control.

Second, you must have a commitment to your marriage if you want to avoid temptation. Have pride in your marriage and family unit.

Commit to building a protective fortress of privacy, love and devotion around them. Have a long-term vision of your life and loving respect for your spouse not just as your husband or wife, but as a human being.

As importantly, make a commitment to yourself – to honor and stand by the vows you made to another person.

The third way to avoid temptation is to have practical strategies that you can use to stop falling into temptation. This may include being aware of your "triggers." Different people have different triggers that will make them vulnerable to temptation.

One person may be triggered by a fear of aging, while another may be triggered by boredom. One may be triggered by insecurity or disappointment, another by loneliness or resentment. Triggers are very subjective. You can usually determine these triggers when working through the question of, "Why did you do it?"

Once these triggers are identified, a couple must work together to manage them in a holistic and collaborative way in the marriage. This doesn't mean the wayward partner is absolved of responsibility for, or ownership of, his or her untrustworthy behavior. It just means that couples who work as allies to manage their respective triggers tend to have happier, healthier marriages than couples who don't work as a allies.

Although many couples find their own strategies to avoid temptation – and I encourage you to do so – I will offer a handful of strategies here that I think are particularly valuable. Take them, leave them, or amend them to your preference or lifestyle. Do whatever works for you.

• Don't put yourself in compromising positions. If you find your secretary attractive, don't stay late after work to talk to her about her mean boyfriend. If you find your neighbor attractive, don't invite him in for a coffee when your husband is at work. Practice self-restraint and good judgement before sexual excitement has a chance to entrench itself or compromise your judgment. The best way to resist temptation is to avoid it altogether.

• Limit opposite-sex friendships. In most instances, it isn't necessary to exchange personal phone numbers with your personal trainer or opposite-sex co-worker. There's really no valid reason to be texting or communicating via social media with these kinds of people. Doing so only increases the chances that an "innocent" opposite-sex friendship will escalate into something more. Spend your time and energy on your spouse and kids instead.

• Pause and then fast-forward. Temptation is a "rush." It happens in a rush, too. That is, people who give in to temptation often say that they felt "swept away" by the whole thing or that "it just happened so fast." So slow down! When you feel the first stirrings of temptation, hit the "pause" button to slow down the entire process. Then, fast-forward and ask yourself: *What will happen if I continue down this path? What will happen if I stop this thing in its tracks right now, and call my spouse instead?* You know which future outcome is better. Pause and think about it. Sometimes that in itself is enough to derail the runaway train of temptation.

• Use more empowering self-talk. Instead of saying, "I can't give in to the temptation of talking to this person," say "I don't flirt with women who aren't my wife." There's a big difference between the rather weak-sounding "I can't" and the stronger-sounding "I don't."

• Make fidelity your identity. Instead of thinking, "I shouldn't be texting this person," think "I'm not the kind of person who does things behind my spouse's back." Make sexual and emotional fidelity your identity – a part of who you are as a person – instead of just regarding it as a behavior. Find pride in your character and choices.

• Replace the face. This isn't just a rhyme, it's a great strategy. When you find yourself in the presence of a person who appeals to you, when you feel your arousal or desire start to stir, picture your partner's face instead of the tempter's face. Use sheer force of will to do this if you must. If you begin to imagine yourself in a sexual situation with the temper, instead imagine yourself in a sexual situation with your spouse. Channel the excitement to a better place and person.

• Practice self-control in a holistic way. It sometimes happens that a person who demonstrates poor self-restraint in their sexual life also demonstrates poor self-restraint in other areas of their life, whether it's losing their temper or drinking excessively. If that resonates with you, commit to working together, as a couple, to improve your overall lifestyle. If a wayward partner can learn to have greater impulse control in other areas of his or her life, it will be easier for him or her to practice greater impulse control in terms of his or her sexual behavior.

It may seem that this content about avoiding temptation belongs in Part II, for the spouse who broke trust. However, I've included it here for both partners since at any time in a marriage either partner may be faced with temptation.

Having an anti-temptation attitude and strategies in place can help both partners avoid falling into the trap of temptation.

The Role of Forgiveness

Forgiveness is a beautiful, liberating thing. It is the ultimate goal when recovering from infidelity or broken trust. It lets both partners get on with life and it frees their minds, hearts and spirits of painful memories that keep them stuck in the past.

Forgiveness will absolutely be necessary – at some point in time – if the marriage is to fully recover from the breach in trust.

You'll notice that I said *at some point in time.* That point in time does **not** need to be in the immediate aftermath of an affair or infidelity. Stay with me here.

Too often, I see forgiveness being "forced" upon a betrayed spouse. That is, he or she is pressured by his or her partner, counselor, friends or family, even society itself to forgive the wayward spouse.

The message is that you can't begin to rebuild until you have truly and completely forgiven your partner for his or her betrayal.

That is untrue. You can begin to rebuild, even if forgiveness is not yet in your heart or mind.

Often, forgiveness is held out as some kind of divine state of being. "To err is human, to forgive divine." Betrayed spouses are told that they should forgive their partner and that, once they have done this, peace will descend upon them.

They are told that healing cannot happen until they feel true and complete forgiveness or give the "gift" of forgiveness to their partner.

This puts *waaaaay* too much pressure on a betrayed spouse, at least in the immediate post-infidelity period. He or she may be nowhere near feeling true forgiveness; however, he or she may still be fully willing and able to move forward in the marriage in good faith, toward recovery and healing.

Forgiveness isn't necessary to make the decision to remain in the marriage and work on it.

I'll let you in on a little secret. Couples who are struggling with infidelity are a challenge for practitioners like me to work with. They are emotional. Wayward spouses present with their own set of high emotions, but betrayed spouses can be particularly difficult to manage.

They cry and have emotional outbursts. They are unpredictable and may rage. They may clam up and withdraw. The heartache and anxiety can be oppressive, and it can be hard to feel like you're making any progress with these folks.

Worse, clients often expect "results" super quick. If they don't feel you've helped them after the first session, they may be dissatisfied with your services.

As a result, it is common for counselors, coaches and therapists to "push" forgiveness on a couple. Why? Because this puts the burden on someone else – specifically, the betrayed spouse.

The goal of some counselors is to have the betrayed spouse wear the crown of forgiveness because, to be brutally honest, it calms them down. It makes them easier to work with. It creates an artificial aura of acceptance and forgiveness.

And when that happens, a couple is easier to manage. They themselves may think their problems are solved. What a miracle worker the counselor is!

The problem is, this only works in the very short term. Betrayed spouses who are pressured to forgive too soon, before they have processed what has happened and come to terms with it, will soon cough up the very "forgiveness" they have been asked to swallow.

A person can only suppress his or her true feelings for so long. Unfortunately, those true feelings – "Hey, I don't actually forgive you yet!" – can come back stronger than ever, as if they're making up for lost time. The whole thing can backfire to delay healing and progress.

My point is this: don't get caught up in the idyllic or theoretical idea of forgiveness. Don't think that it is some kind of divine "state of grace" that a betrayed spouse can simply "will" into being or feeling.

I've seen struggling couples become almost obsessed with the idea of forgiveness. They focus on it so much that they stop moving forward and their healing grinds to a halt.

Some betrayed spouses will even think there is something wrong with them because they cannot yet forgive their partner. They may question the loving foundation of the marriage: "If I truly loved my spouse, shouldn't I be able to forgive him/her?"

At the same time, some wayward spouses become wounded or unduly concerned by their partner's lack of quick forgiveness. "If she/he doesn't forgive me now, maybe she/he never will." They may also grow impatient or anxious, saying things like: "You need to forgive me" or "I can't go on until you've forgiven me."

All of this creates a destructive and utterly unnecessary point of contention between two people who are already struggling.

In this way, the *concept* of forgiveness becomes a barrier to *actual* forgiveness. Talk about shooting yourself in the foot!

Please, do not do this. True forgiveness is too important. Your marriage is too important.

If you're a betrayed spouse who doesn't yet forgive your partner, that's okay.

As long as you have made the conscious choice to move forward in your marriage with an open mind and heart, as long as you are committed to doing the work it will take to rebuild, you're on the right track.

As long as you are not deliberately withholding forgiveness as a form of punishment, control or martyrdom, it's okay if you don't feel it just yet.

If you're a wayward spouse who has not yet heard the words, "I forgive you," don't panic.

Don't assume this is the end or that forgiveness will never come. Don't excessively "beg for forgiveness" or expect your spouse to forgive you on your timeline.

In some ways, forgiveness is like trust. Both are feelings that may take time to develop or re-develop after an indiscretion. Both are feelings that may that require "proof" in the form of a wayward spouse's future actions and behaviors.

While some people can quickly forgive or trust again, other people need more time.

My advice is this: If true or complete forgiveness has not happened at this point in time, you should focus instead on embracing *the spirit of forgiveness* by behaving in ways that will help your relationship heal.

Keep your nose to the grindstone. When forgiveness does come – and it will – it will be all the sweeter. And your marriage will be stronger for it.

The Importance of Having a Passionate Marriage

You've probably heard the expression, "The best defense is a good offense." This is known as the strategic offense principle of warfare. The general idea is that taking a proactive stance to defeat your enemy, rather than passively waiting for your enemy to attack, is more likely to result in victory.

As it is in war, so it is in marriage. A couple who proactively nourishes emotional and sexual intimacy, as well as fun and friendship, is more likely to overcome – and avoid – infidelity than a couple who waits until a trust issue arises before doing anything about it.

Be vigilant. Work together, as a team, to have a romantic friendship. Work together, collaboratively, to have a passionate marriage. Model for your children what a loving, long-term marriage looks like. Remember that you are spirited lovers and best friends who truly enjoy each other's companionship, not mere roommates who are sharing the bills out of convenience.

In the words of Germaine Greer, "A successful marriage requires falling in love many times, always with the same person." If I had to limit my marriage advice to one sentence, that would be it.

A passionate marriage has an arsenal of weapons at its disposal. A satisfying sex life, one where both partners show enthusiasm and focus on the other's pleasure in bed. Good communication. Positive, easygoing and friendly interactions. Humor. Appreciation, acknowledgement and humility. Devotion. A sense of history and a long-term vision of a shared future. Strategies to avoid and resist temptation, if and when it arises. Patience. Perspective. An insatiable curiosity about each other.

I could go on, but you get the idea.

Yes, infidelity does happen in marriages that are otherwise happy and healthy. That is especially so today with the prevalence of personal technology, something we have already discussed in this book.

Yet there is no doubt that infidelity finds it easier to sneak up on a passive marriage than a proactive one. There is no doubt that it's easier to inflict damage on a passionless marriage than on a passionate one.

So build that fortress around your marriage. And then when it's built, climb to the top with your spouse and stay alert for anyone who tries to get inside. If you can see them coming, and if those walls are solid enough, there is no way they can cause any damage to the life you've built together.

A Final Word to Readers

Despite the hardline I often take with couples and the many struggling marriages I have seen up close and personal, I am still a hopeless romantic. I believe that two people can stay married for life and that their lives, and the lives of their kids, are richer for it.

You've chosen this book because you're going through one of the biggest challenges a couple can face. I hope that you have found strategies herein that will help you rebuild trust and construct a stronger fortress of love, devotion, happiness and friendship around both your marriage and your home.

I would encourage you to return to this book often, even during those times your relationship is strong. Flip through its pages to keep its insight, strategies and focus fresh in your mind.

However, if after reading this book you still feel that you require in-person couples mediation or counselling, I encourage you to keep a few things in mind as you seek out professional help. Be sure to choose a practitioner who is married, who does not have a hidden religious agenda (a spiritual aspect is fine, as long as you are aware and accepting of it) and who works exclusively with couples (is not a generalist). You have every right to ask these questions.

If you are facing more serious problems in your relationship (i.e. abuse, addiction, mental health issues, personality disorders, anger issues), I advise you to, without delay, seek out a practitioner who has special training in these areas. Find the right person for the job.

I will leave you with my best wishes for you and for your family.

Sincerely,

Debra Macleod, B.A., LL.B.

ABOUT THE AUTHOR

Debra Macleod, B.A., LL.B., is a marriage author-expert, couples mediator and leading resource for major media in North America. Her top-selling books are sold worldwide and have been translated into several languages.

Debra's Marriage SOS book series:

Marriage SOS:
30 Lifelines to Rescue Your Relationship in One Month

Marriage SOS:
Blended Family Edition

Marriage SOS:
Oilpatch Edition

Visit Debra's private practice at MarriageSOS.com

"There is no remedy for love
but to love more."

- Henry David Thoreau